ANSCAR VONIER: ABBOT OF BUCKFAST

ABBOT VONIER AT THE TIME OF THE CONSECRATION OF BUCKFAST
ABBEY CHURCH

ANSCAR VONIER

ABBOT OF BUCKFAST

*

WITH SOME ACCOUNT OF THE
RESTORATION OF THE ABBEY
AND ITS CHURCH

By

DOM ERNEST GRAF

Monk of Buckfast

THE NEWMAN PRESS
WESTMINSTER, MARYLAND

B
V

Visa attestatione censoris a Nobis deputati, permittimus ut opus cui titulus: 'Anscar Vonier: Abbot of Buckfast', a Rdo. P. D. Ernesto Graf conscriptum, typis mandetur, si caeteris, quorum interest, ita videbitur.

D. WILFRIDUS UPSON, O.S.B.
Abbas Visitator.

Datum in Monasterio
S. Mariae de Buckfast,
die 30a Novembris 1956

NIHIL OBSTAT: JOANNES M. T. BARTON, S.T.D., L.S.S.

CENSOR DEPUTATUS

IMPRIMATUR: E. MORROGH BERNARD

VICARIUS GENERALIS

WESTMONASTERII: DIE XX FEBRUARII MCMLVII

PRINTED IN GREAT BRITAIN

First published 1957

COELI MUNDIQUE REGINAE

BUCKFASTRIAE PATRONAE

MUNUSCULUM

DEVOTIONIS ARGUMENTUM, AMORIS PIGNUS

CONTENTS

vii

ILLUSTRATIONS

PREFACE

ST. MARY's Abbey church of Buckfast is undoubtedly Abbot Vonier's most enduring memorial. His boundless faith and trust in divine omnipotence and human generosity brought the dream of his monastic youth to glorious fruition. As long as that noble building stands on its medieval foundations the name of the second abbot of the new Buckfast will defy the passage of the years. So it would seem superfluous to write a 'Life' of a man who needs no other memorial: *Si monumentum quaeris, circumspice.* But there were many who thought otherwise.

On the very day of the Abbot's funeral, Lord Clonmore, who represented the firm of Burns and Oates at that sorrowful yet uplifting solemnity, spoke to me about a biography of the deceased prelate, and in *The Month* the late Fr Keating—a great friend of the Abbot—also expressed a hope that a 'Life' of so remarkable a man would not be unduly delayed. However, for various reasons, no attempt was made to meet this demand. For one thing, we were too stunned by the suddenness of our bereavement. Eventually Abbot Bruno Fehrenbacher, Dom Anscar's successor, pressed me to undertake a task which I felt to be beyond my capacity. It may well be that the reader will agree with me at least on this point. However, I made a start some ten years ago, but again and again the work was put aside for long periods at a time, until the beginning of 1956.

Many people probably imagine that a man like Abbot Vonier must have left a quantity of papers, diaries, letters and such-like documents, which form the basis of a sound biography. But in this respect I found myself at a great disadvantage. The Abbot left no such documents, with the sole exception of a number of letters addressed, over the years, to the Lady Abbess of St Scholastica's Abbey, Dourgne, Tarn, France. These letters have been carefully preserved, and were very kindly put at my disposal by the present Abbess. They have been an invaluable help in my task. The Abbot's sister, a nun of the Assumption at Auteuil, Paris, also fortunately kept her brother's letters, but most of them are only short notes. For all that they are precious documents for, as Newman observes, letters are 'that kind of literature which more than any other represents the abundance of the heart, which more than

any other approaches to conversation' (*Historical Sketches*, Vol. II,
p. 221). I have accordingly made the most of these letters for in them
we hear an echo of a loved voice.

It may be useful to offer a word of explanation of the seemingly
uncalled for digression after the very first chapter of this book. Such a
digression was necessary for a proper understanding of the history of
the new Buckfast and of the rôle played in its restoration by Abbot
Vonier. This story has never been published, except in the pages of the
Buckfast Abbey Chronicle, but the circulation of that modest periodical
is exceedingly limited. My account of the way in which 'the dry
bones' came back to life is based on the *Annals* of the Abbey, viz. the
record, from day to day, of the various events and incidents that make
up the tapestry of life in a monastery. For the more spectacular occasions
I have drawn on the files of the newspapers in addition to the aforesaid
Annals. For a fuller account of the rebuilding of the Abbey, as well as
for its past history, I may refer the reader to the excellent, illustrated
Historical Guide to Buckfast Abbey by Dom John Stéphan. This book,
though small in size, is much more than a 'Guide' and represents the
study and research of many years.

It only remains for me to thank the Editor of *The Tablet* for permission to quote from the files of that invaluable source of information; also Messrs. Longmans for permission to quote from Abbot
Butler's *Benedictine Monachism*, and especially the house of Burns and
Oates, the publishers of Abbot Vonier's works. I have freely quoted
from the *Collected Works* of the Abbot published by them in three
volumes a few years ago. In all quotations the Roman numerals refer
to the volume, the Arabic to the page.

CHAPTER I

CHILDHOOD AND EARLY VOCATION

Exi de terra tua . . .

IN a world in which 'not a hair of our heads shall perish', and in which the life and death of the ubiquitous sparrows are the personal care of the Maker of the distant galaxies, it was surely no whim of blind chance that wafted the youthful Martin Vonier from a small village in rural Swabia to a no less rural corner of 'the sweet South-West' of England. When we ponder the splendid career of this imposing figure of a modern monk, we are bound to say *Digitus Dei est hic*, with as good reason as Pharaoh's wise men of old.

In the course of the very year that was to be his last on earth, Abbot Anscar set down in writing some of his meditations on the working of divine Providence.[1]

When one reflects upon this remarkable essay in the light of his own career the impression is forced upon the mind that much of it is auto-biographical, even though unconsciously. 'When we speak of God as preparing anything, we mean more than the watchfulness of the Creator of all things over His handiwork; we think of the Almighty in terms not only of foresight and foreknowledge, but of active pre-occupation. He has already in hand the business whose conclusion will not be seen till the fulness of time has arrived, till the preordained hour has struck.'

The life of the man who wrote those lines is a striking illustration of their truth; it is also a startling demonstration of the accuracy of his observations on the working of this great law of the moral order. 'It is in the very nature of preparation,' he writes, 'that at no time should the hand of God be withdrawn from the clay which it is slowly moulding into its predestined shape.' Of old, Israel's inspired singer prayed thus to the Lord: 'Let Thy Hand be upon the man of Thy right hand, and upon the son of man whom Thou hast confirmed for Thyself.'

[1] *The Clergy Review*, January 1938, 'Divine Preparations'.

Rarely did prayer of this kind meet with a more magnificent answer than in the career of Abbot Anscar. One of his most attractive traits was a reasoned optimism. In his person this most enviable disposition, which often enough stems from no higher principle than rude health or a shallow mind, was born of an unlimited trust in, and childlike reliance upon, the hand that had guided him from the days of his youth.

A good home and a sound Christian upbringing give a man the best possible start in life. This double blessing the future Abbot enjoyed in fullest measure. His own views on this matter may be illustrated by an incident slender enough in itself, yet by no means insignificant. One morning, at a time when he was acting as assistant to the novice-master, though not yet a priest, the present writer told him how much he had been struck by a well-known passage of the Book of Wisdom which had been read at Matins that night, viz. the text: O quam pulchra est casta generatio cum claritate. 'That text,' Dom Anscar observed, 'does not by any means bear the meaning which you attach to it; it refers to the immense boon it is for a man to spring from a good, sound religious stock.' The exegesis was perhaps questionable, and a novice must not argue even with an assistant novice-master, but it reveals the trend of his mind at that time.

In spite of the French appearance of his name and the French pronunciation of it that he adopted when he became Abbot of Buckfast, Anscar Vonier had not a drop of French blood in his veins. His family migrated to Germany from the Tirol, that most profoundly Catholic of all the various provinces of what was once the Austrian Empire. His cradle stood in the small Swabian village of Ringschnait, but his parents moved to another village situate at no great distance from the ancient imperial town of Biberach, when he was only a few years old. Besides cultivating a fairly extensive farm, his father also owned a brickworks. The future Abbot was one of fourteen children, and since he was born on the feast of St Martin, 11th November 1876, he was given the name of that great wonder-worker of the West.

At an early age the boy began to serve in the sanctuary of the village church. Many a priest, when surveying the road that led him to the steps of the altar, will probably find that these lowly, yet very sacred functions were for him one of those divine preparations of which the Abbot wrote so feelingly. They surely were in his own career. Another such preparation may have been the pilgrimages he sometimes made in company with his devout mother to the ancient Benedictine abbey church of Ochsenhausen. The spacious abbey buildings, once peopled by monks, now house an agricultural school, but the magnificent baroque church still serves its original purpose, though only as a secular parish church. At this period, viz. in the eighties of the last century, there were still alive men and women whose parents had seen the monks in their choir stalls, for the 'secularization' of the monastery only dated from the first decade of the century. Whether these visits, and the circumstance that he grew up on land that had actually been the abbey's property—a fact of which he was well aware—gave rise to the first stirrings of a religious vocation in the heart of the youthful pilgrim, it is impossible to say, for though I often heard him speak of these pilgrimages, and always with obvious delight, he never gave a hint about his impressions. However, silence in one who scarcely ever spoke of himself neither proves nor disproves anything. One effect of these visits, however, must have been some sort of mental picture of the monastic life. Moreover, a home such as that of the Vonier family would not be without that portentous volume popularly known as *Legende*, which contained the 'Lives of the Saints' for every day of the year. In those days it was a universal custom, after the evening meal, for father or mother, or one of the older children, to read aloud to the assembled family the story of the saint of the day. Since so many saints were either monks or nuns, it was easy to acquire at least a rudimentary notion of the religious life even though there was not a single monastery of men in the land.

The law permitted indeed the existence of some convents of nuns, but these were tolerated solely because the inmates were given to education, nursing or other charitable activities. Hence, when a youth in the kingdom of Württemberg wished to embrace the religious life, he was perforce obliged to leave his country. The law was iniquitous, but even here we may see a divine preparation—a very remote one it is true, yet one that led to the momentous decision which eventually brought to the scene of his life's work the man whom we can only think and speak of as the second founder of Buckfast Abbey. The revival of the religious life at Buckfast and the reconstruction of the monastery church on the ancient foundations has been described by some as a 'romance', while others have spoken of it as a modern 'miracle'. We shall surely not be far out if we view so unusual an event as a singular proof of God's good will towards this country and as a token of future blessings for a kindly, naturally religious people which, though robbed of its rightful inheritance, contrives to cherish a vague, romantic regard for the ancient monastic Order which it knows to have been so closely linked with its religious and cultural life.

At this stage the reader may justifiably ask how it came about that when a young foreign boy left home and country in order to follow what he felt to be the call of God, he should have come precisely to this remote spot in the South-West of England. An answer to this query will necessitate a somewhat lengthy digression, but unlike the usual digression, what now follows is an essential part of the story of Abbot Anscar's life and achievement, while at the same time it will recall certain painful incidents in the religious history of France and Germany during the nineteenth century.

CHAPTER II

FRANCE'S LOSS, ENGLAND'S GAIN

THE beginnings of Buckfast are shrouded in the mists that obscure so much of the story of the last decades of the first millennium of our era. However, we know for certain that by the middle of the tenth century monks had established themselves in what was then a lovely and secluded valley.[1] Here then, to the accompaniment of the murmurous mountain stream which trips so gaily over stone and boulder on its way to the not very far-off sea, at first Anglo-Saxon monks, and, a century or so later, Normans as well, lived their quiet, uneventful but far from unfruitful lives of prayer and praise of the Creator. Though withdrawn from the world, these early monks of Buckfast, like their dedicated brethren all over Europe, proved to be the world's best friends and benefactors. Of no set purpose and, as it were, by accident, they preserved all that was best in the civilization of Greece and Rome, while by the labour of their hands they reclaimed the wilderness and taught a rude people the arts of peace. They were men of prayer first and foremost, in obedience to the axiom laid down by the father of Western monasticism—*Nihil operi Dei praeponatur*—nothing may supersede or displace the worship of the divine Majesty. But St Benedict also coined another axiom, viz. that idleness is an enemy of the soul. Thus it came about that prayer and work constituted the woof and the warp of their dedicated existence. One might have thought that normal people would greatly value such an institution. Actually they did—until the middle of the sixteenth century, when there came to the throne of England a king who proved to be 'a blot of grease

[1] I had just corrected the last of the galley proofs of this book when Dom John Stéphan's years of research into the story of Buckfast were unexpectedly rewarded by an exciting discovery among the Estate Papers of Lord Petre, recently entrusted to the care of the Devon County Archivist. From these documents we learn that 'King Cnut, at the instance of Duke Aylwarde, first founder of the said Abbey (of Our Lady of Buckfast) in the year of Our Lord God 1018 . . . who founded the said Abbey in pure almoyn requiring but only prayer, and included the lands in the same writing . . .'

This is the first definite statement discovered up to date concerning the name of the founder and the date of foundation of Buckfast as a 'Benedictine Abbey'. Other items in the same Papers suggest that there was some sort of religious establishment on the spot from King Edgar's time.

and blood on the pages of English history'. Then were the voices of God's minstrels hushed and the sanctuary lamp quenched in this valley. No longer in the long winter nights were the wayfarer's eyes gladdened by the distant glow of the windows of the great church; no longer could the poor and the ailing knock expectantly at the monastery door. Silence and desolation brooded over the hallowed spot, and if a stray wanderer, gazing upon the fragments of altar and statue, pillar and wall that cluttered the ground, asked himself, 'Shall these dry bones live again?' his voice would die away with the murmur of the nearby stream. Three hundred years more went by, but then, upon a mellow autumn day, other monks, few in number it is true, and speaking in accents which those who had once dwelt here would not have understood, came to take possession of the deserted spot. The dry bones were about to come to life, and this is how it came about.

In the year 1880, and in the years immediately following, France was undergoing one of those anti-christian convulsions which have so often shaken her frame and of which the religious Orders were invariably the first victims. All over the country monasteries and convents were being suppressed and their inhabitants expelled, sometimes by sheer brute force, and the buildings assigned to profane purposes. One of the houses thus rudely suppressed was the Abbey of La Pierre-qui-Vire, founded only a few decades earlier by a man who had lived and died in the odour of sanctity. After a few years spent in the ranks of the pastoral clergy, P. Jean-Baptiste Muard went through a formal noviciate with the Trappists of Aiguebelle and at its termination made his religious profession as a Benedictine. With a few companions of a spiritual calibre not unlike his own, the new Benedictine settled in the midst of a vast forest in an isolated district of Burgundy known as Le Morvan. In spite of the extreme austerity of the life, or perhaps because of it, men soon flocked to the very primitive monastery, with the result that within a few years of the premature death of the saintly founder a large abbey and a fine church modelled on the famous basilica of Vézelay replaced the rustic bungalow that had done duty as monastery and church in the founder's lifetime.

But all too soon there dawned another fateful fifth of November. On 29th March 1880, the chamber of deputies passed a law which empowered the government to suppress all such religious establishments as failed to secure what was called 'authorization'. Not that the authorities had the slightest intention of granting such a favour. The government was further empowered to use physical force in the event of the victims refusing to leave their homes of their own accord. The iniquitous law called forth the indignation of all right-minded people, and that not only in France or in Catholic circles. It is pleasing to record that the *English Church Union* sent a message of sympathy to Cardinal Guibert, Archbishop of Paris. In its issue of 27th November 1880, *The Tablet* printed the text of a letter in which the Cardinal expressed his thanks to the president of the E.C.U., the Hon. C. L. Wood, who was none other than our good friend and neighbour, the late Lord Halifax, who paid us many a visit whenever he happened to be in residence at his country house at Bovey Tracey.

The execution of the law did not proceed as smoothly as its authors had perhaps anticipated. The expulsions were sometimes marked by revolting scenes of violence, when appeal had to be made to the *gendarmerie* and, as at La Pierre-qui-Vire, to the armed forces of the Republic. The story is well worth rescuing from oblivion, all the more so as it is organically connected with the story of Buckfast.

On the morning of 5th November 1880, darkness lingered long over the forest of Le Morvan, now stripped of its gold and amber foliage. That forest makes of La Pierre-qui-Vire an island of peace, where silence reigns eternal, a silence enhanced rather than broken by the soughing of the wind and the gurgling of the brook that meanders past the rocky platform on which the monastery stands. That morning, as on every other morning, the monks had risen early from their hard pallets, but whereas on other days they might try to snatch an hour's sleep after the night Office, if the cold which comes early to that upland plateau made sleep possible—on this night the priests said their Masses as soon as Lauds were over, and all the Brothers received Holy Communion. They needed the food of the strong, for mischief was afoot in the darkness without.

The community had unanimously resolved to ignore the summons to quit spontaneously what was their rightful home—they would only yield to force. Upon the use of force the authorities accordingly decided. On the previous day, a Friday, the *préfet* of the Department of Yonne had arrived at Avallon for the purpose of superintending in person the final preparations for the inglorious expedition of the morrow. However, when he demanded the co-operation of the *procureur* and his assistant, M. Bazin and M. Moreau, both these gentlemen refused. 'I am a magistrate,' M. Bazin declared, 'as my father and my grandfather were before me. I refuse to disgrace my office—I resign it.'

If the monks enjoyed but little sleep that night, the *préfet* was kept out of bed altogether. At two o'clock in the morning, by which time the servants of God were at prayer in their choir stalls, the representative of the Republic set out from Avallon accompanied by a locksmith, a carpenter, a posse of gendarmes, and, for good measure, a platoon of fifteen soldiers from the regiment stationed at Auxerre. The official plan was to carry out the deed quietly and without rousing the Catholic population. It was similarly resolved, nineteen centuries before, that a certain arrest was to be made quietly: *Non in die festo, ne forte tumultus fieret in populo.* History *does* repeat itself! But the monks' friends were not without means of information. The secret had leaked out, with the result that, in spite of the darkness and the cold of that early winter's morning, there was gathered within the precincts of the abbey a considerable number of priests and laymen, the latter headed by that great Catholic gentleman, the Comte de Chastellux, who had been the community's friend and generous benefactor from the first days of the foundation.

Meanwhile the expeditionary force, not unlike another armed band of long ago, was tramping through the chilly night, for the plan was that they should reach their objective before daybreak or, at the latest, by first light. The commander-in-chief, that is the *préfet*, had set up his headquarters at a convenient distance from the scene of action, in the village of Saint-Léger-Vauban, the birthplace of Marshal Vauban, Louis XIV's famous military engineer, a man who, but for the interest taken in him by some Carmelite friars, would probably have died in the obscurity of the village which has since added lustre to its name by linking the marshal's name with its own. Five o'clock had struck when the gang arrived before the main gate of the monastery. They found it bolted and barred against them. The commissary of police then read the *préfet's* order in a loud voice and summoned those on the other side to open the gates. The Abbot—Dom Bernard Moreau—was a very sick man at the time, so it fell to Dom Etienne Denis, his eventual successor, to act in his name. This venerable and saintly man—Buckfast's first superior—refused to comply with the summons on the ground of its illegality. He took his stand on the fact that he was the legal owner of the place and in the full enjoyment of all the rights and privileges of a free citizen of the Republic. The community's solicitors lodged a similar protest. All was in vain. Orders were given to batter in the stout outer gates. The heavy blows of the carpenter's axe were punctuated by cries of '*Vivent les Pères! Vive la religion!*' As soon as a breach had been effected, the invaders rushed through the gap, only to find themselves before yet another heavy door, the one giving into the monastery proper. This also was battered in by the carpenter's axe.

While these inglorious operations were in progress in the inner court of the monastery, the monks locked themselves in, every one of them in his own cell, so that when the gendarmes swarmed up the main staircase, they were obliged to smash in each individual door. The first cell they came to was occupied by P. Eugène Ménétrier. 'I am seventy-two and have spent forty years in this cell. I am not going to quit.' 'That is nothing to us,' the men answered.

P. Eugène was cast in heroic mould, a giant of a man and endowed with a powerful voice. When on his return from some preaching engagement he was asked how he had got on, he would playfully observe that he had preached 'avec une voix de tonnerre'. He hailed from a place called Tonnerre—Thunder!

When the gendarmes came to the Prior's room they found themselves face to face with the Comte de Chastellux as well. On this fateful morning that noble friend did all in his power to help and comfort his friends, especially the aged and the sick. One of the latter, Père Jennades, firmly refused to leave his cell—he would only yield to force. As the agents of the government were about to lay hands on him, he protested that he still held a captain's commission in the army, that he had fought at Gravelotte, and for that reason he was entitled to an escort of two gendarmes. It pays, on occasion, to stand on one's dignity! The monk got his escort of two, but when they reached the head of the staircase the old man observed, with a significant motion of his hands, 'It's a good thing for you fellows that I am a monk, otherwise you would go down before me!' One presumes that the descent would have been more speedy than dignified. When the men came to the cell of Fr Edmund Boussard, who died at Buckfast at the age of ninety-three, that saintly man also refused to leave: 'I am here by the will of God,' he protested, 'no one shall make me leave this cell.' So he too was forcibly dragged out.

Five of the monks were in the infirmary. The officer in command announced that only four could be permitted to be ill, since only four had been allowed for in his instructions! One of the five was called Albéric. On hearing this name, an exotic one to his ears, the officer asked if a man with such a name was not a foreigner. 'A foreigner!' P. Etienne exclaimed: 'Why, the man is an ex-sergeant and an old campaigner in Algiers—and he is now seventy-two years old.'

While these disgraceful scenes were being enacted within the monastery, the soldiers guarded all the issues so as to prevent anyone from re-entering the house. When all were finally gathered in the inner court of the monastery they formed a procession which went first to the shrine of the Sacred Heart which dominates the entrance to the abbey. From there the procession wended its way to the statue of Our Blessed Lady which, some years before, had been erected on the ancient dolmen from which the place got its name—La Pierre-qui-Vire. The dolmen consists of two superimposed circular stones of huge dimensions, like two millstones, the upper one of which, according to popular belief, was wont to turn on its axis at the sound of the Angelus. Hence the name La Pierre-qui-Vire. There they stood, before the great statue, the gift of that distinguished writer Montalembert, the historian of the monks of the West. With tears in their eyes and voices strangled by emotion, they sang a farewell hymn to the Queen of heaven and earth. But if there were tears in their eyes, there was hope in their hearts. Tyrants come and go, they and the mischief they do are but incidents which the Church—and monks—take in their stride. Like the oaks of the forests amid which they so often choose to dwell, monks outlast their persecutors, and when driven from their holy retreat they have a knack of returning as soon as the storm has blown over—or they find as good elsewhere. On the Sunday before this outrage, these men, for whom the Church's liturgical prayer was daily food and inspiration, cannot have failed to note a prophetic hint in the words of the Introit of the day: *Ego cogito cogitationes pacis . . . et reducam captivitatem vestram de cunctis locis.*

By a singular coincidence—if that is the right word—this same text was the Introit of the Mass on Sunday, 29th October 1882, which was the first day after the monks' arrival at Buckfast, though the Sunday Mass was displaced by that of the Patronage of Our Lady which was observed on that Sunday before Pius X's reform of the calendar. However, at this moment the community's plight was pitiful enough. It is not very likely that on that morning any of them, however vivid their recollections of schooldays, would remember the immortal poet's words which so admirably describe their condition:

Diversa exilia et desertas quaerere terras
. . . . agimur . . . .
Incerti quo fata ferant, ubi sistere detur.

For the time being they needs must disperse. Some of them repaired to their own homes, or to the houses of friends, while one group—a considerable one—made for the coast and the ever hospitable shores of this island which has always gloried in sheltering the victims of persecution, whether religious or political. On their arrival in London they were met by Dom Edmund Luck, the future Bishop of Auckland, who shepherded them to St Augustine's Abbey, Ramsgate, where they were received with truly fraternal charity. However, it was evident that their stay could only be a temporary one. Now it so happened that at this time the community of Ramsgate owned extensive property at Leopardstown, on the outskirts of Dublin, which would provide ample accommodation for the exiles. Accordingly, after a few days' rest they took to the road once more. They landed on the shores of the Emerald Isle on 28th November, but now they were accompanied by one of the Fathers of Ramsgate, the late Dom Adam Hamilton, who had most generously volunteered to throw in his lot with the French exiles. Of this remarkable man more will be said in the sequel.

At this day Leopardstown is a household word in racing circles. There, some years previous to the arrival of the French monks, an Irish monk of Ramsgate had opened an agricultural school for the sons of gentlemen. The undertaking proved a failure, for a number of reasons which have nothing to do with this story. Its failure threw a heavy financial burden on the Ramsgate community. At this time the sole occupant of the premises was Dom Oswald Monti, who was assisted by a lay brother known as Brother Patrick, but whose canonical status was somewhat ill-defined. Dom Oswald's position was likewise exceedingly precarious. In the words of the first annalist of Buckfast, 'he was forced to have recourse to all sorts of expedients to maintain both himself and the place'. This remark is devoid of any sinister implication, it is a characteristic sample of the literary manner of the chronicler of that period, Dom John Baptist Garnier, who spoke and wrote as no one else did. His memory deserves to be rescued from oblivion for he rendered great service to this community over a number of years. He was a native of the cathedral city of Troyes and entered at La Pierre-qui-Vire when already in Holy Orders. At Buckfast his duties as cellarer brought him in daily contact with tradespeople and workmen, with whom he was extremely popular by reason of his straightforwardness. If he was satisfied, he said so, but he made no mystery of his displeasure if there was occasion for it—so everybody knew where they were. He was tall, thin, endowed with a good singing voice, and a good exponent, though somewhat mechanical, of Gregorian Chant as understood and interpreted in those remote days. He had a phenomenal memory for facts and dates. It used to be said that he could tell you how many cannon shots were fired at the battle of Waterloo, for he was particularly well informed about Napoleon and his campaigns. I was too young to form a true estimate of this extraordinary man, but even the youngest of the boys in the alumnate could not but be impressed by his exemplary regularity and the charity and kindliness for which his office provided so many occasions. On Sunday afternoons he used to give us an hour's religious instruction. To this we looked forward as to one of the most interesting events of the whole week, for he made that hour a period of sheer delight and we were free to question him on all sorts of subjects. On the other hand he lacked a saving sense of humour, and perhaps for that very reason provided not a little amusement for other people. Even to us boys in the alumnate his speech seemed affected and unduly pompous: he would have been an immense success in the Circumlocution Office. 'It has seemed good to the Holy Ghost,' he would say, 'to do so and so, but He might have done differently.' Men were usually described as 'sons of Eve' and women as 'daughters of Adam'. This particular idiosyncrasy appeared to give him great pleasure. Human respect did not enter into his composition and he was utterly indifferent to what people might think or say. This could be embarrassing. I recollect being taken to the doctor by him. At the entrance to the nearby town he produced a large rosary and bade me recite the *Paters* and *Aves* aloud as we walked up the main street. It was even more disconcerting to have to enter a shop with him, for he would address the man or woman behind the counter with some ponderous formula, such as: 'This servant of God requires a pair of shoes' while he pointed to the shrinking figure beside him. Yet with all his quaintness he was the kindliest of men. About the year 1900 he transferred to St Augustine's Abbey, Ramsgate, where he acted as novice-master up to the time of his death in 1912.

At the time of the French monks' arrival, Leopardstown was a quiet district, hence very suitable for the kind of life contemplated by the newcomers. The name suggests a zoological garden, but the place had never housed leopards or any other wild animals. It is almost certainly a corruption of 'lepers' town', which arose from the circumstance that at one time there had been a lepers' hospital there. This surmise is borne out by the discovery of several mass-graves dating, it would seem, from periods of high mortality among the inmates of the establishment. Leprosy, now happily unknown in Europe, was long endemic all over the Western continent.

From the first day of the monks' arrival the regular monastic routine was resumed with all the rigour of La Pierre-qui-Vire, which, though the religious wore the black habit of the Benedictines, did not to all intents greatly differ from that of a Trappist monastery. In the spring of the following year there were five professions and even an ordination by the Archbishop of Dublin, the future Cardinal McCabe. On this occasion the sacristan was unable to produce either tunic or dalmatic for the sacred ministers. Such a *contretemps* would have broken the heart of an orthodox master of ceremonies, but, if rumour may be trusted, Frenchmen are not lacking in personal initiative in matters of ritual and ceremonial. With the approval of the officiating prelate— no less enterprising in this respect—the deacon and subdeacon respectively donned the light silken tunic and dalmatic which the archbishop should have worn under his chasuble.

CHAPTER III

THE MONKS RETURN TO BUCKFAST

THE exiles soon realized that they could not remain permanently at Leopardstown, were it only that the property was heavily mortgaged and the creditors were taking steps for its sale, while on his part the Archbishop denied them all parochial rights in the district. As a matter of fact the acting Superior, Fr Thomas Dupérou, had already toured the country in search of a suitable house—but all in vain. This was the moment when Providence—through our premier Catholic newspaper—intervened in signal fashion. A periodical such as *The Tablet* needs no praise from the pen of the present writer, but it is no exaggeration to say that, humanly speaking, but for *The Tablet*, Buckfast Abbey might still be the not very impressive residence of a country gentleman—it would have been too small for a school or hospital—and tourists and trippers might occasionally come over from Torquay and elsewhere, to have a look at what remained of the 'Abbot's Tower' and a few walls, window or door jambs, and fragments of tiles. That there is so much else and so much better to see is undoubtedly due, in part, to *The Tablet*.

One September morning Fr Adam Hamilton was reading his *Tablet*, as he had so often done before. He was the only member of the community who could read it in those early days. Suddenly he leaped from his chair in a state of considerable excitement. There, in the correspondence columns of the paper, was a letter the writer of which suggested that in view of the fact that just then a number of expelled communities were seeking asylum in England, it would be a grand thing if one of them were to acquire an old monastic foundation in the West of England, viz. Buckfast Abbey, which happened to be in the market at the time. The owner, as explained by the writer, was a Protestant, but for all that he was anxious 'that the place should again come into the hands of the Catholic Church, and he would agree to very liberal terms in treating with any Order who would become a purchaser'. The letter was signed 'Brother Lawrence', no doubt on the strength of the writer's being a Dominican tertiary. At that time, Mr Henry Raddall, of Launceston, was a married man, or perhaps already a widower. At a later date he came to live at the Abbey as an oblate and for a number of years discharged the onerous duties of a door-keeper. He also acted as guide to visitors, but in those days these were few in number and the duties of a cicerone were practically only a summer occupation.

The Tablet, therefore, was the instrument of Providence in the recovery for the sons of St Benedict of one of the oldest though not the largest or the most famous of the ancient houses of our Order in this country. There were others who also played a rôle in the good work, some of them a purely negative one, as when the Dominicans, after looking at the place, decided that it was unsuitable for their purpose. Let me quote Brother Lawrence once more: 'One morning', he writes, 'I was at Bishop's House, Plymouth, having a yarn with Fr Matthews, a priest who afterwards left the Church and got some schismatic bishop to give him episcopal consecration. Fr Matthews was telling me of Buckfast Abbey, of which I had never heard before. He told me that the property belonged to Dr Gale, of Lockyer Street, who was thinking of selling it. I went up and saw Dr Gale, and after chatting together for some time he handed me some papers and views of the place. Then I set to work writing to different communities all over the country, asking their prayers that the place might come into religious hands. Among others I wrote to the Dominican Sisters in the Isle of Wight.[1] In a few days I had a reply from one of the Sisters, who wrote in the name of the Prioress and said how very pleased they all were at what I had told them, and asked for further information. They appeared most interested in the place and would, I think, have liked to settle there themselves.' We can all of us be grateful for the good Sisters' prayers while thanking God for not answering them in the way they were perhaps meant. Brother Lawrence continues: 'I was greatly edified by their [the nuns'] interest. . . . Being a tertiary of the Order I wrote to the Provincial . . . the Provincial did not think there was much chance of their being able to take Buckfast, but he assured me he would bring the matter under the consideration of the Chapter which was to be held a few weeks later. The members of the Chapter did not think the place suitable for their purpose. After this I happened to meet Fr Amherst, S.J., who was giving a retreat to the

[1] That is, the Sisters of the Convent of Carisbrooke, I.O.W., who are strictly cloistered.

Sisters of Notre Dame, and he advised me to write to *The Tablet*.' He did so, with the result everybody knows.

As soon as he had read the letter in *The Tablet*, Fr Adam hastened to the Superior's room. Fr Dupérou's mind was made up instantly. Without losing a day he and Fr Adam sailed for Plymouth to interview Dr Gale, a man who had attracted public attention as an inventor, all the more so as he had been blind from the age of seven. The two monks were most kindly received by Dr William Vaughan, the Bishop of Plymouth. An inspection of house and grounds fully satisfied the Fathers and before long all the formalities for the renting of the estate for a period of seven years, with the option of purchase within a period of two years, were completed. The purchase was actually effected in June of the following year. The price agreed upon for house and estate was £4,700.

On 28th October 1882, at eleven o'clock in the morning, an advance party of seven monks reached Buckfast. A second batch arrived in November and the rest followed in December. The cellarer has left it on record that the total cost of the migration from Ireland, including the packing and shipping of furniture, amounted to 3,200 French francs.

On 28th October, Holy Church honours the Apostles SS. Simon and Jude. That year the day was a Saturday, the day which modern piety has set apart for the special honour of the Mother of God. That night Compline was recited in what had been the drawing-room of the private residence and which had been hastily turned into a chapel. Thus, after a gap of three and a half centuries, a new choir of monks took over where their predecessors had left off. To human shortsightedness three centuries seem a very long time indeed, but in the perspective of history they are but an incident. In any case, monks, like the Church, think in centuries. Persecution, violent uprooting, exile and fresh starts are only passing episodes in the life of men whose profession has on it the patina of antiquity and is, as it were, tinged with the changelessness of eternity.

On the following day, Sunday, the Church observed the feast of the Patronage of the Blessed Virgin Mary. Thus it came about that the first Mass celebrated amid the ruins of Mary's sanctuary, after a lapse of three and a half centuries, was offered in her special honour. This first Mass, said by the Superior, was a Low Mass, but at nine o'clock there followed a *Missa Cantata* at which the celebrant was Fr Adam. Those who knew this remarkable and most lovable man can have no difficulty in imagining the tremendous emotion that must have swept over his sensitive mind and heart, and the happy tears that surely bathed his radiant countenance, for, like a very great personage of our own days, Fr Adam would weep unashamedly under stress of strong emotion. The annalist records that they had no harmonium to support the voices: 'We sang what we could, that is, the *Kyrie*, *Gloria*, *O Salutaris*, and *Salve Regina*—such was our first sung Mass here.' Musically and liturgically the mixture was an odd one, but how the spirits of the monks of old must have exulted in the abode of bliss as they listened—for surely all heaven was agog that morning—to the identical words and the very same melodies they themselves had once chanted on this blessed spot! In the evening there could be no Benediction of the Blessed Sacrament owing to an awkward mishap. When the priest came to the altar he was unable to open the small tabernacle which they had brought from Ireland. 'Thus,' the annalist writes, 'Jesus was a real captive in His voluntary prison and the priest had to withdraw as he had come.'

By All Saints' Day the situation had improved. On that day they had a proper liturgical *Missa Cantata*, although at Benediction the celebrant only wore a surplice and stole—they were as yet without a cope. On the third Sunday after their arrival three people from the outside world attended Mass. One of them was an old Irishwoman, the only Catholic in the whole district and who, in consequence, had practised her religion only spasmodically. There were mitigating circumstances in her case since the nearest Mass-centre was a private house at Totnes, seven miles distant, and there were no Sunday trains. The other two were Army officers on holiday in the neighbourhood. On Christmas Night fifteen people, all of them Protestants, were present at the Midnight Mass. By this time monastic life was going on as if no untoward incident had ever interfered with its regular course.

Early in December of that year the venerable bishop of the diocese paid the newcomers the first of many fatherly visits. It was in keeping with that prelate's love of simplicity that he should arrive unannounced and at the kitchen door. For a moment the Brother cook took him for one of the tradesmen. At two o'clock in the afternoon the whole community gathered in the oratory, where they sang the *Magnificat* and the hymn of St Benedict, after which the bishop gave his blessing and immediately departed as informally as he had come. From the day of the monks' arrival that truly apostolic prelate had taken the liveliest interest in their affairs, aware, as he no doubt was, of the immense possibilities thus opened for the revival of the ancient faith in this part of Devon, though neither he nor anyone else could have foreseen the extraordinary developments that the coming years were to bring forth.

Those were the heroic days in the life of the community—days of great hardships, privations and ever-increasing toil. Meals had perforce to be eaten in the place where they were cooked and, owing to an inadequate supply of spoons and forks—knives were not needed since they abstained from flesh meat—they were compelled to eat in relays, packing-cases doing duty as tables and chairs. St Benedict's Rule was observed to the letter, hence everybody took his turn in the kitchen. This strict adherence to the letter of the Rule occasionally led to results which, in retrospect, make us smile, but which, at the time, were probably less mirth-provoking. The late Bishop Graham, Bishop Vaughan's secretary and eventual successor, who used to accompany that venerable prelate when the latter held ordinations, delighted in relating what happened on the day of the ordination to the priesthood of Dom Boniface Natter, Buckfast's first abbot. Chance would have it that the ordinand was also the cook of that week. On the great day someone else officiated in his place, but with dire results, for when dinner was served, the fish was found to be raw on one side and burnt on the other. It was perhaps fortunate that they ate no meat in those days.

Fr Adam Hamilton, the only Englishman (no! he was an ardent Scot!), constituted the providential link between the monks and their neighbours in the village. Fr Adam's was an outstanding personality. By his geniality and the persuasive eloquence of his words he cast a spell upon all who had the good fortune of coming in contact with him. Sprung from an ancient Scottish family, he was born on 14th August 1841 and embraced the religious state at an early age. After his noviciate and profession at Subiaco, he went through a brilliant course of studies at the Roman College, where he took his doctor's degree of theology. It is characteristic of this saintly man's modesty that no one in the community ever heard of this academic distinction. I have known him almost all my life, and had him for my professor of theology, but I only learnt the above detail when I read his obituary notice. When the French refugees arrived at Ramsgate, Fr Adam begged to be allowed to share their fate, thereby exchanging the peace and assured tranquillity of a well-established monastery for the trials and hardships inseparable from a new foundation. But for him, humanly speaking, the French refugees at Leopardstown might never have heard of Buckfast. In this first period of the story of the new Buckfast, as well as in the sequel, Fr Adam rendered to the community services worthy of undying remembrance. He possessed all the qualities that make the orator—a beautiful, strong, melodious voice, a lively imagination, as well as a keen intelligence and a tenacious memory, and there was a warmth in the tone of his voice which rendered his words irresistible. Both his written and spoken word had about it an old-world charm and dignity which reminded one of no one so much as Cardinal Newman. Let this passage from a letter to friends and parishioners suffice as an example. After thanking them for their gift of money towards the church building fund, he wrote: 'There is yet one thing I cannot forbear to speak. Around this fair vale there has for a thousand years hovered in a mysterious way the special protection of the Mother of God. It is the first of England's valleys hallowed of old by her protection that has again become her sanctuary by the building up from the ruins of one of her consecrated dwelling-places. Why she chose it among so many we cannot tell, but shall one day know.' This was written not many days before his death and, besides being a sample of his beautiful literary manner, it is his supreme expression of his love for Buckfast. One of the outstanding features of his spiritual character was his intense love for the Mass. Up to within a few days of his death, when scarcely able to stand, he would drag himself to an improvised altar near his room, supported by the infirmarian. 'As long as I can say Mass,' he used to say, 'I shall value life.' He was called to his reward on 12th December 1908, four days after he had celebrated the golden jubilee of his monastic profession. His last, or almost his last words, were an echo of Our Lord's own words on the cross: 'I commend my soul to God.'

As the dry bones came to life and the community got into its stride, the monks became increasingly conscious of what the ancient Romans called the *genius loci*, that is, in the present instance, of the impressive fact that they were on historic and very sacred ground. Manual labour had its place in the daily routine of the choir monks as well as in that of the lay brethren, so once a vegetable garden had been got under cultivation, the most obvious as well as the most fascinating task they could engage in was the exploration of the soil under their feet. No visible relic of the ancient church and monastery remained, with the exception of a fifteenth-century, ivy-clad tower, now known, no one knows why, as the 'Abbot's Tower'. After a good deal of fumbling, the ancient foundations of monastery and church were eventually found and the task of removing the four to five feet of earth which covered them was at once taken in hand. At the same time the need of more domestic accommodation was being painfully felt. Above all there was a pressing need for at least a temporary church. It was decided to erect such a building on the south side of the above-mentioned tower. This tower consisted of a basement and three stories, the floors of which had of course collapsed. After extensive restoration, the two upper stories were turned into chapels, the lower one became the sacristy, while the basement was made a museum in which were stored such relics of the past as had come to light in the course of the exploration of the site.

The foundation-stone of the temporary church was laid on 11th July 1883. The architect was none other than Bishop Vaughan himself, while the cost of the construction was borne partly by the community and partly by a few generous benefactors. The cellarer noted that the total expenditure amounted to just under one thousand pounds. The bishop declined an architect's fee—the community's prayers, he declared, would be ample reward.

From an aesthetic point of view the new church was disappointing enough—it could scarcely be more commonplace—but it served the community well, over a long period, and with the passage of the years it seemed to acquire a spiritual atmosphere which it is easier to sense than to define. For the older members of the community it holds sweet and sacred memories since most of them were professed, or ordained priests, within its walls. That humble sanctuary was the scene of the blessing of the first Abbot of Buckfast since the Reformation as well as of that of the subject of this book. It was not without a twinge of regret that some of us exchanged the homely, well-loved edifice for the striking but somewhat chilly splendour of the new Abbey church. The old church now houses our books and thus retains power to raise the mind to higher things.

The return of the monks to Buckfast was an event of considerable interest, not for themselves alone, or for the immediate neighbourhood, but for the whole of Catholic England. Catholics were not slow to perceive that here was a heaven-sent opportunity to undo, at least in some measure, the harm done by those who had wrought the destruction of the monasteries, and to rekindle on this spot a light which the chill blast of the Reformation had apparently quenched for ever. At an early date a committee was formed for the purpose of raising funds for the reconstruction of the whole Abbey on its ancient foundations. The committee was headed by the Duke of Norfolk and included some of the most illustrious names in contemporary Catholic life, such as those of Cardinal Newman, Bishop Ullathorne, Bishop Hedley, W. S. Lilly, and Dr St John Mivart, who acted as honorary secretary. The correspondence between Dr Mivart and Cardinal Newman on this subject is preserved at the Birmingham Oratory. In his first letter, dated 30th October 1883, the Cardinal wrote: 'My dear Professor Mivart, I thank you for your interesting letter, and rejoice to be told that the old Benedictine abbey is to revive. I gladly would give my name to your committee of restoration at once, but for the want of information of the relation of the French Benedictines to other houses in this country already. If the Bishop of Birmingham associated himself with the exertions of the committee, that would remove my difficulty.

'Also I should say that, my means not being very ample, what I have to give away I feel to be best expended upon objects, Catholic or local, of first importance; and this leads me to ask myself whether there would not be an inconsistency in me giving my name to an object calling on the public for contributions, and not furthering it by my example.'

Professor Mivart replied that 'the matter we are interested in has its national, antiquarian and artistic, as well as its religious interest. Your Eminence is a Prince of the Church but no one is more an *Englishman*, and it is rather to the learned and refined Englishman than to the Ecclesiastical Prince that the appeal is made. . . . I have recently visited Downside and heard how well the monks of Buckfast were spoken of there. . . .' On 11th November 1883, the Cardinal wrote: 'I shall be happy to have my name placed upon the committee for the restoration of the Abbey.'

The prime mover and supporter of the whole scheme, however, was Lord Clifford of Chudleigh, who, from the first, proved the most generous friend and benefactor of the community. His name will be for ever linked with the second foundation of Buckfast Abbey, as also the names of his two immediate successors to the title. With a view to perpetuating the memory of the Abbey's happy association with the noble house of Clifford, and as an enduring reminder of the immense debt of gratitude we owe to it now as much as in the past, Abbot Natter prayed Lord Lewis, the 9th Baron Clifford, to allow his arms to be quartered with those of Buckfast. Mr. Frederick Walters, a promising young architect and a convert to the faith, was chosen as architect. Mr Walters was more than an architect of distinction; he was also a well-informed antiquary and a keen numismatist. He threw himself into the work with youthful enthusiasm and in the course of the years became a popular, greatly loved figure among us. A small stained-glass window under the western gallery of the new church shows him on his knees in prayer. It was a happy inspiration to depict him in that attitude, for he was a deeply religious man and an ardent and most intelligent lover of the Church's own prayer—the Liturgy. After the first opening of the Abbey church in 1922 he invariably spent Holy Week and Easter with us, when his piety and obvious appreciation of the solemn functions of the Great Week were an inspiration for the community.

Building operations on the south wing of the monastery began in the autumn of 1884. It was not intended, at first, to erect the south cloister, though the omission would have entailed no small inconvenience for the community. However, in the course of the following year, on the occasion of one of his periodical inspections, and realizing the inconvenience, Lord Clifford instructed the architect to draw up plans for this cloister and to erect it at his sole expense. At a later period, his son bore the whole expense of the erection of the east cloister, while at a still later stage, his nephew and heir, the Hon. Charles Clifford as he then was, erected the north cloister in memory of his young wife, who died prematurely during the world-wide epidemic of the year 1918. Thus those three cloisters, which impress the beholder by their dignified simplicity, constitute an abiding memorial to the noble house whose kindness and warm-hearted friendship towards the community has been and still remains as unfailing as it is unostentatious.

The Bishop of Plymouth had been pressing the Fathers for some time to erect a small house on the site of the south aisle of the old church in order to provide accommodation for the novices, but they were reluctant to spend money on what would necessarily be only a temporary building. However, in the end they yielded to the good prelate's pressure. They did so all the more readily as he arrived one day with a complete plan and a contractor's specifications. Building operations began while work on the south wing of the monastery was still in progress. The cost of the new structure was £304, a figure that may convey a fair idea of the architectural features of a structure which happily has long ago ceased to disfigure the landscape. Unbeautiful though it was, the house proved exceedingly useful. For a number of years it housed both the novices and the boys of the alumnate—at least the boys' study-room occupied one half of the ground floor. Bishop Vaughan personally paid the contractor the sum of £120 and at the same time informed the community that this sum was a loan without interest. In November of the same year he wrote to say that the community need not think of ever repaying it.

One reason, perhaps the main one, of the Bishop's interest in this temporary dwelling was his fear lest the efforts of the committee for the restoration of the Abbey should fall short of what was hoped for. However, at a later date he gladly acknowledged that the result had exceeded his most sanguine expectations. At this time, too, Père Etienne Denis, who was now Abbot of La Pierre-qui-Vire and, of course, Superior of Buckfast, decided to build the west wing of the monastery up to the first floor. This structure was roofed in with corrugated iron, with the result that the rooms—viz. chapter and parlours—were exceedingly hot in summer and bitterly cold in winter. I need hardly say that at this period there was no question of central heating—in fact, the mere suggestion of such a thing would have been regarded as a scandalous pandering to the modern world's love of comfort.

The early spring of 1886 saw the completion of the south wing. It was inaugurated with due solemnity on Easter Tuesday, 27th April. The celebrations began with a Pontifical High Mass sung by Bishop Vaughan. At its conclusion a noteworthy sermon was preached by one of the bishop's many clerical brothers, Dom Jerome Vaughan, Prior of the Scottish Abbey of Fort Augustus. The preacher chose for his text the prophetic words wrung from Balaam as he looked down upon the hosts of Israel: 'How beautiful are thy tabernacles, O Jacob, and thy tents, O Israel' (Num. xxiv. 5). This tribute to Israel by the blear-eyed old charlatan and unconscious prophet is an admirable description of the surroundings of this Abbey and a prophetic forecast of the untold blessings showered upon this privileged spot and, surely we may add, radiating from it.

In due time a large company met in the new refectory for a repast seasoned with speeches both numerous and eloquent. Lord Clifford said that he remembered wandering as a boy amid what was left of the ruins of the Abbey, twenty years before this day. Little did he then think of what was to take place so soon on this spot, or of the event he had witnessed that day. His pleasure in the work that had been done, and which he trusted would be continued, was enhanced by the fact that the Abbey rested on its ancient foundations—that he was, he

3

might say, in the old refectory, and that the work had been so done as to afford an accurate and faithful representation of the monastery that stood here centuries ago. Many years later the present Lord Clifford told me how his uncle, Lord Lewis Clifford, had more than once told him that when his father first took him to see the ruins of Buckfast he told him—as by a prophetic instinct—that the day would come when he would have a great deal to do there.

One incident must not be omitted. The lunch in the refectory on the day of the opening of the south wing was not the first meal to be partaken of in the new refectory. On the previous evening, as was surely their right, the monks themselves had inaugurated the stately hall. But they had done so after their own fashion by partaking of a supper consisting of bread and water and eaten upon their knees.

CHAPTER IV

MARTIN VONIER COMES TO BUCKFAST

At the period described in the last chapter, all the members of the Buckfast community were Frenchmen, with the sole exception of Dom Adam Hamilton and two young clerics, that is, choir monks not yet in priestly orders, who were natives of Germany. A few years before the expulsion from La Pierre-qui-Vire, these two strangers had been admitted to the alumnate of the French abbey. As the spectre of eviction began to loom ever larger on the horizon, these youths were entrusted to the care of the Holy Ghost Fathers of Beauvais, where they continued their study of the humanities at the Fathers' college. These two youths were none other than the late Dom Wilfrid Schneider, who, amid great exertions and hardships, founded the now flourishing mission of Totnes and secured the present temporary church, formerly a non-Catholic Sunday school; and the future abbot Dom Boniface Natter.

The presence of these young Germans in a French community was but another of those divine preparations of which this story provides more than one instance.

From the very beginning of the little community's life at Buckfast, the question of its survival—that is the problem of recruitment—became an actuality, even though not a pressing one—at least for the moment. There were those for whom Buckfast was only a temporary asylum. As soon as the anti-religious storm should have blown itself out, they would return to France. Fortunately, there were others, above all there were Fr Adam Hamilton and the Bishop of Plymouth, who insisted on its being made perfectly clear to all the world—and in particular to the French religious authorities—that the monks had come to stay. As a matter of fact, in view of the wonderful charity and good will with which they had been received, it was unthinkable that there should ever be a day when, of their own free will, they would pack up and leave so hospitable a country.

However, several years were to pass before anxiety on this score was completely and finally allayed. In December 1898, Cardinal Dominic

Serafini, at that time Procurator General of our Congregation in Rome, paid us a visit of a few days. It was in the nature of things that he should also pay his respects to Bishop Vaughan, then living in retirement at St Augustine's Priory, Newton Abbot. It appears that before the aged prelate would engage in conversation he insisted on his distinguished visitor giving him a solemn pledge that in no circumstances would the monks be withdrawn from Buckfast. That pledge was readily given, for so retrograde a step had never been contemplated in the most authoritative quarters. But this incredible notion was only finally scotched when the community of Buckfast was detached from its parent body and given a separate and independent existence. This step was taken in answer to the practically unanimous prayer of the community in the year 1899. This being so, the problem of survival had to be tackled, but a solution was not easily come by. On the one hand, ecclesiastical and religious recruiting in France was severely hampered by the universal military service enforced by the laws of the Republic. Moreover, there was little likelihood that an appreciable number of young Frenchmen would feel an urge to migrate to this remote corner of Devonshire. And it must be added that the regime at the time was such as to require not only a keen desire for the religious life, but likewise robust health and a readiness to endure hardships which, in the light of later experience, were seen to be excessive, and to which young boys in particular should never have been subjected.

On the other hand, there was not a single monastery of men in several states of the then recently re-created German Empire—even in those regions where the whole population was Catholic. Fr Wilfrid and Fr Boniface were both natives of Swabia, a very Catholic province of the small kingdom of Württemberg. Their presence in the community drew the attention of Superiors to a vast and fertile field of recruitment. Here was a rich source well worth tapping. Moreover, would it not be poetic justice and the repayment, as it were, of a long-standing debt, if the country and county of St Boniface were to be served and edified by some of those whose forebears had received the light of faith at the hands of one of the noblest figures of English history? This idea may or may not have been decisive, but the fact is that a small school—an alumnate as it was called—was opened for the education of German boys who showed signs of a call to the monastic life and the priesthood. No difficulty was experienced in filling the school. It was enough for Dom Boniface to show himself in his native land for a number of would-be monks to flock to him, so much so indeed that Buckfast became almost a household word in the Swabian parts of Württemberg and scarcely a year went by without one or more fresh arrivals from that Catholic country. But there were likewise many departures, for only a small number stayed the course. Many left of their own accord after a more or less prolonged trial of their strength, while others were gently but firmly bidden to return whence they had come. Of those who left, some joined other institutes or became secular priests. In any case there can be no doubt that all were much the better for their temporary stay in a monastery.

At this stage the reader may well ask by what means Fr Wilfrid and Fr Boniface found their way to La Pierre-qui-Vire, and so to Buckfast. Humanly speaking—hence foolishly—it all happened, as it were, by chance. Actually it was due to the circumstance that of several German girls who went to school at the Benedictine convent of Oriocourt, recently founded by the Abbey of Flavigny, near Dijon, to learn the language, two or three actually became nuns, one of them a sister of Fr Wilfrid. Now it also happened that some of the Fathers of La Pierre-qui-Vire occasionally visited both convents; one of these was Dom Leander Lemoine, himself a native of Lorraine, and who later became one of Buckfast's temporary superiors. To him the young German nun spoke of her brother, who, she said, was absorbingly interested in the foreign missions. The result of these conferences was that one day the boy left his picturesque home in the Swabian Alps for the far-away forests of Burgundy. He was soon followed by the future Abbot Boniface. The action of these two youths was fraught with enormous consequences. For a number of years nearly all the professed members of the community came out of an alumnate almost exclusively composed of German boys. However, as I have just said, it must be admitted that the number of those who 'made the grade' was not very large. As a matter of fact, between 1884 and 1917, when the last of the alumni entered the novitiate, 132 boys had passed through the alumnate. Of this number, seventy-five became priests or religious in other Orders, or secular priests, others returned to their own families. For this there were many reasons, the chief one being the excessive strictness of the life. It may seem incredible, but it is a fact that the daily routine of the alumnate scarcely differed from that of the monks, except that the boys did not attend the night Office! They rose, however, at 5.15 all the year round. The system had one advantage—but only one—if you held out until the time came for the canonical novitiate, you knew exactly what you were in for. But the life of growing adolescents had about it a sternness and an unnatural severity the mere recollection of which perhaps still causes the few who stayed the course to shudder even at this time, and to wonder how they stuck it. I have always thought that Dom Anscar's health was grievously injured at that early stage and that it was the realization of it that inspired his subsequent action as Abbot.

The rule adopted by Père Muard was a mixture of the Trappist, Benedictine and missionary ideal—but the Trappist element was certainly its chief ingredient. It is quite possible that if P. Muard had lived another decade or so, he would have realized that these mutually exclusive elements would not blend; but he was unable to put his ideas to the test of time—the only one that is really decisive in matters of this kind. At a much later period, when experience had ripened his judgment, it took all Abbot Anscar's kindness, wisdom and strength of will to establish some equilibrium between the ideal and the humanly possible. The monastic life is by its very nature a stern and even austere discipline; hence the most ordinary wisdom demands that, as St Benedict puts it in his Rule, all things should be so arranged that the strong may wish to do more than is asked of them, while the weaker ones need not be frightened off. The wisdom of Abbot Anscar's action was to be justified up to the hilt in the sequel, for whereas up to the time of his abbacy many came and few stayed—mostly because they were physically unequal to the regime that had come from La Pierre-qui-Vire, at the time of the Abbot's premature death the community was a strong body, nearly two-thirds of its members being natives of the soil, actually not a few of them Devonshire men.

We must now take up the story of young Martin Vonier. In 1887 Dom Boniface Natter's health left much to be desired. It was thought that the best cure would be to send him to Germany to breathe his native air. At the same time he was commissioned to look out for a few suitable boys for the alumnate. In that year the brother of Fr Dunstan Götz happened to be curate to the parish priest of Rissegg, young Martin's home. Dom Boniface called on this good priest, who invited him to come to the village school to speak to the boys about his monastery. The result of the talk was that young Martin and five other lads expressed their readiness to accompany the youthful monk to his far-away monastery. However, there was no room just then for such an influx, nor would there have been adequate facilities for their education. It was accordingly arranged that the boys should go to

Beauvais, to the College of the Fathers of the Holy Ghost. There, on 29th November 1888, Martin Vonier made his first acquaintance with the French tongue, which was then, and was to remain for another ten years, the official language at Buckfast. This one year at Beauvais sufficed to lay the foundation for the Abbot's uncommon mastery of the French tongue, but I think it also sowed the seeds of his great love for France and for French spiritual writers. For Bossuet, the immortal Bishop of Meaux, he had an admiration that knew no bounds.

In September 1937 it fell to my lot to accompany him to the last Provincial Chapter of the French Province which an abbot or a delegate of the community of Buckfast was to attend, for at that gathering we successfully petitioned for union with the English Province of the Cassinese Congregation. As soon as the not very exhilarating proceedings at Saint-Benoît-sur-Loire came to an end, we left in order to spend a day or two in Paris at the Convent of the Assumption, where the Abbot's sister was a nun. We had a whole day to ourselves, and while I visited Chartres, the Abbot made provisional arrangements with Thos. Cook for an excursion to Fontainebleau. However, my greatest wish was to see Rheims and Meaux. When I told him that the train to Rheims was bound to stop at the latter town, he promptly dropped the Fontainebleau scheme. Alas! the train did not stop at Meaux. But when we approached the city the Abbot jumped up and stood at the corridor window for as long as we could see the cathedral tower. 'Nous sommes chez M. de Meaux', he said, using the seventeenth-century style for a bishop, while his whole being was obviously thrilled even by this fleeting vision of that great man's episcopal city.

But I anticipate. On 22nd August 1889, Martin Vonier arrived at Buckfast. The date is a *dies memorabilis*, as memorable as the date— did we but know it—of the first foundation of Buckfast, for on that day the second founder of this abbey finally reached the scene of his future, most glorious activity. At the end of four years in the alumnate, Brother Martin entered the novitiate, where he was given the name by which countless thousands have come to know him. A year later, on 2nd July 1894, he pronounced his perpetual vows. There followed the quiet, uneventful years during which he applied himself to the study of philosophy and theology while at the same time he acquired the habits of prayer and the solid though not glamorous virtues which make the true monk. Before long, though only a cleric, he was chosen to act as assistant to the novice-master, who was also the Superior of the house. In those days it was the invariable custom of the novitiate and clericate to begin the day's work by saying the *Veni sancte Spiritus* on one's knees and in the same attitude to read a few verses of Holy Scripture. For a number of years Dom Anscar invariably read the Hebrew Bible at that time; in fact, the Hebrew Bible was always on his desk. It was by this faithful reading of the Scriptures that he gained that exceptional familiarity with the sacred text which was so marked a characteristic of his preaching and writing. It is not too much to say that he had St Paul's epistles practically by heart. The novitiate library reflected the general poverty of the house, but on its shelves there stood the *Triplex Expositio* of St Paul's Epistles by an old French Capuchin, Bernardine of Picquigny—better known, I think, by his latinized name of Piconio. Dom Anscar had made a thorough study of these volumes, which he regarded as the best introduction to the Epistles of St Paul. I, for one, shall be eternally grateful to him for having put these most valuable, now but little known, volumes into my hands at the very beginning of my studies.

All who knew Abbot Anscar were struck, and sometimes non-plussed, by his taciturnity. He was a man of few words and more willing to listen than to talk—a characteristic which, it has been said, earns for a man a reputation of being a good conversationalist! In his younger days, however, he was much more communicative. On 17th December 1898 he was raised to the priesthood by the Bishop of Plymouth. His outstanding intellectual gifts as well as his solid religious spirit were recognized by everybody. It would have been a pity if one so richly endowed were not given opportunities for those higher studies which Buckfast was unable to provide. He was accordingly sent to our Roman college on the Aventine. He came back at the end of one scholastic year after obtaining a doctor's degree within that short period. For those who knew Dom Anscar previous to his Roman studies there can be no doubt that the year spent in such a setting marked a real crisis in his life. He came home with a deeper and what, for lack of another term, I might call a more catholic notion of the monastic ideal. At Sant' Anselmo he had met men, both young and old, who were as keen and enthusiastic Benedictines as he, but whose ideals and actual practice differed considerably from what he had assimilated at home. He was wise and open-minded enough to per-ceive that even as not any one particular religious Order is a full repre-sentation of our Lord's earthly life, so no particular house, or group of houses, may claim to be completely representative of the ideal of St Benedict. We only grasp that ideal in its full richness when, by a generous sweep of the mind's eye, we take in all the various families that are the spiritual offspring of the patriarch of the West.

Dom Anscar's Roman experience was to stand him in good stead when only six years later he was called upon to assume responsibilities weightier than those of a professor in a monastic school, or the various subordinate offices which came to him as soon as he returned from Rome. In the last months of 1902 Buckfast was once more raised to the canonical status of an abbey, and Dom Boniface Natter was duly installed as Abbot on St Matthias' Day 1903, a year of years to the very day since the surrender of the house into the grasping hands of Henry VIII by the last Abbot of Buckfast, Gabriel Donne. Abbot Natter, then in the full vigour of mature manhood, was an able man, but his gifts lay in the practical rather than in the speculative sphere. It was surely a remarkable tribute both to his character as a man and to his ability as an administrator when, in 1906, the abbots of the French Province chose him—a German—for the position of Visitor of that widespread Province. In this capacity Abbot Natter twice crossed the Atlantic. In midsummer 1906 he was due to make a canonical visitation of a monastery in the Argentine Republic. For such an act the Cassinese Constitutions prescribe that the Visitor be assisted by a *socius*. It so happened that in the previous year Abbot Boniface had been constrained to yield to the persistent demand of the Abbot Primate that Dom Anscar should come to Sant' Anselmo to teach philosophy. He had completed the first of the five years for which he had been lent to the college. The long vacation had come, so the choice of a co-Visitor was easy, all the more so as his health left much to be desired. For some years already Dom Anscar had been a victim to frequent bouts of violent headaches which completely incapacitated him for any kind of work for several days at a time.

A few years later, in a letter to the Abbess of Dourgne dated 18th October 1912, he refers to his ill health and complains that even the Lady Abbess 'lays the blame for my bad health on myself', though she, of course, 'does so infinitely more gently than some others'. He writes: 'Since 1903 my life has been nothing but a long chain of physical misery—I might almost say moral misery, for the seat of the illness is in my head. In Abbot Boniface's time I could never take food without my head being as it were poisoned. During my last year [viz. before he went to Rome] I had thought of a remedy—I ate nothing at dinner [at midday in those days] but drank a bowl of tea. Rome did me an enormous amount of good. After that. . . .' The sentence is left unfinished. 'The day before my blessing [as Abbot] I felt so bad that I was unable to receive my guests. At that moment I should have taken a six months' holiday. In these circumstances, you will say, it was folly to undertake more than was strictly necessary. I agree; but if I had not chosen the period of Abbot Boniface's death to start my work, his death would have profited us nothing—*sa mort nous aurait été inutile* [*sic*]. As for philosophizing—for me that is my only human comfort.' The sentiment in the last sentence obviously shows that he regarded Abbot Boniface's tragic death as a sort of immolation, and those who knew Abbot Natter cannot but feel convinced that his last conscious act would have been a prayer that God would accept the sacrifice of his life for the good of the religious family to which he was so devoted. That this was Abbot Anscar's conviction appears from a letter of 20th December of the same year: 'I have suffered more [in the course of that year] than in all the previous thirty-four years of my life [*sic*], and what I learnt before all else is that a man can pretend to no greater dignity than to be the Lord's instrument in His secret plans. . . . It is a strange thing, but the longer I go on, the more I feel, in the depths of my heart, Dom Boniface encouraging me to carry out his work, which is a work of the future even more than a work of the present hour.' Prophetic words, surely, for us who have lived to see the fruits of the first Abbot's sacrifice and the second Abbot's labours. The few members of the community whose memories date back to those days cannot have forgotten the uncanny feeling, the real though unreasoned anxiety that somehow got hold of us when we learnt that the voyage to South America was not to be made on an English ship. The Abbot was aware of our feelings, but when we spoke of our anxiety he tried to laugh it off. Was our disquiet a foreboding of impending tragedy? The fact remains that, however uncalled for it may have seemed, there was real disquiet in our hearts. The Abbot had twice crossed the Atlantic in the three previous years, but on those occasions no one had ever experienced similar emotions. All too soon our anxiety was to be justified by a catastrophe which, while it cut off the first of the new line of Abbots of Buckfast at a time when he was only getting into his stride, also put an end to any dreams of a professor's career Dom Anscar may have cherished up to that fatal Saturday afternoon of 4th August 1906.

On 8th July Dom Anscar wrote to his sister in Paris from Genoa, where he was spending a few days after leaving Rome. Brother and sister had been looking forward to a happy meeting and Dom Anscar was keenly aware of his sister's disappointment and of her not unnatural concern at the prospect of so protracted a sea-voyage. After explaining the reasons for the journey, Dom Anscar wrote: 'Superiors have judged fit that I should spend the long vacation by acting as *socius* to the Abbot Visitor and to spend three weeks at sea and one month on *terra firma* near the South Pole [*sic*]. At the moment I am at Genoa enjoying the sea-breeze morning and evening and bright sunshine in between. If you deem it appropriate to wish me *bon voyage* you must make haste. But before all else it is clear that in addition to the opportunity for a big sacrifice which this order of my Superiors provides for us, you have a weightier motive than ever to discharge your loving duty towards your poor brother.

'I am not thinking of shipwrecks; but the thought of two periods of three weeks, each without being able to say Mass [the sentence is left unfinished]. Then the prostration caused by the heat of the regions we shall be traversing! However, we are in God's hands, and as for me, I shall always have a place in the heart of my sister. But what an egoist I am—always talking about myself. I should have begun by asking how you are yourself.

'We are very small creatures, aren't we? What I should like at the moment is to be transformed into a little fish so that I might plunge into this lovely Mediterranean Sea and remain there for ever, so as to escape from the heat and, to some extent, from my own self. You will say that this is not a very lofty aspiration; but the fact is that one would be ready to be metamorphosed into frogs rather than remain what we are. But we have Him who is for our souls the great Pacific Ocean, as St Catherine of Siena was wont to call God. Meanwhile I'll make a pilgrimage to St Catherine of Genoa. May God's will be done in us.'

A few weeks later he wrote once more, this time from Spain: 'For over a week I have been in the land of St Teresa. Unfortunately, Avila is too far from here [he was writing from a monastery in the Pyrenees] for me to realize one of my ambitions—that of seeing the places consecrated by the presence of the great Saint. . . . So as not to waste my time I am learning Spanish since I am in the country where they speak this tongue of the Angels. . . . I'll send you a line as soon as I get to Buenos Aires, in order to reassure you about my fate and to let you know whether or no the sun of the tropics has caused me to melt like butter. *Au revoir*! then, dear Sister, sooner or later.'

Little did he foresee that they were to meet within a very few days after his tremendous ordeal in that azure Mediterranean Sea in which, a short while ago, he had longed to float.

CHAPTER V

SHIPWRECK AND RESCUE

ABBOT BONIFACE and Dom Anscar met at Barcelona on 3rd August and embarked on the same day on the Italian steamer *Sirio*, which had sailed from Genoa on the previous day, having on board 750 Italian emigrants bound for South America. The ship's complement consisted of 118 persons. The vessel had been built at Glasgow in 1883. Nothing unusual occurred on the first day and the next, a Saturday, until the middle of the late afternoon. The day was a perfect summer's day and the sea as calm as the proverbial mill pond. The ship was proceeding at full speed when suddenly, at about three o'clock, she struck a submerged rock just off Cape Palos and within sight of the coast. Perhaps one of the best accounts of the ensuing catastrophe is that of the Spanish newspaper *Heraldo*, which was widely reproduced by the British Press. This account is based on the report of the skipper of the French steamer *Marie-Louise*. 'The *Marie-Louise*', we read, 'doubled Cape Palos yesterday (4th August) and was making for Alicante. When a few miles away we saw the Italian steamer *Sirio* crossing our course at full speed. I was pointing her out to a shipmate on deck when, to my surprise, she came to a sudden stop. I trained my telescope on her for I felt convinced that something untoward must have happened. I knew that there was a shoal north-east of the Hormigas Islands and that the *Sirio* was passing directly over the spot, so I could only conclude that an accident had befallen her. My surmise was confirmed when I saw her bows rise out of the water and her stern go down. . . . I brought my ship round at once and made for the sinking steamer. As we did so we heard a tremendous explosion—the *Sirio's* boilers had exploded! Shortly afterwards we saw bodies floating in the sea and dreadful shouts for help reached our ears. We put on full steam and hastened to the rescue. The *Marie-Louise* remained on the scene of the tragedy until all was over and the sea had closed over the victims. We picked up fifty-four persons.'

Another paper, the *Diario Universal*, gave some further details: 'Immediately after the *Sirio* had struck the reef all the fishing-boats in the neighbourhood hastened to her assistance. The first to reach her were the *Joven Miguel* and the *Vincento Llicano*. The captain of the former acted in a most heroic manner. Running his vessel close to the *Sirio* he took off about three hundred emigrants. As the vessel began to settle in the water, the crew of the *Joven Miguel* wanted to move away, but the captain would not hear of it. "So long as there is a single soul to rescue, we stay here," he said. The *Vincento Llicano* saved two hundred souls. A fisherman who, though lame, manœuvred his own boat single-handed, rescued twelve people.'

As almost always when a disaster occurs at sea, the wildest rumours about the conduct of the captain and crew of the *Sirio* soon began to circulate. It is a fact that the captain was guilty of a grave error of judgment when he set his ship on the course that resulted in its loss, but tales of cowardice or selfishness on his part or that of his crew have not been substantiated.

At a later date Dom Anscar wrote an account of his dreadful ordeal, the sober objectivity of which is far more impressive than the lurid stories of newspaper correspondents writing in haste. Dom Anscar writes: 'About two o'clock in the afternoon—we had not seen land for some time—I descried a lofty promontory—it was Cape Palos. I went down into my cabin, with the intention of returning on deck when land would be nearer. I had not been there for more than twenty minutes and was actually coming up in order to join my travelling companions on deck when all at once I felt as if the ship were being lifted from under my feet and dropped down again. I was thrown on the floor, but rose and rushed out into the passage where I met a steward whose face wore the pallor of death. The tray he had been carrying had fallen from his hands and made its own contribution to the most terrifying clatter of shattered glass I ever heard. When at length I managed to get on deck I noticed that our ship had not only stopped, but that she was on an incline of some thirty or forty degrees to the right. . . . When I rejoined my Abbot he was apparently discussing the situation with the two bishops who were also passengers on the *Sirio*. "Well, what do you think of it?" I asked Fr Abbot. "I don't think it means much", he answered, "provided these people do not lose their heads."

'At this moment a large vessel was seen sailing between the *Sirio* and the Spanish coast, perhaps five or seven miles away, but in the translucent atmosphere of the south it seemed to be very much nearer. The sight spelt hope for me and for everyone else. How could one perish in so beautiful a sea and in sight of a powerful vessel? All she need do was to swing round to be at our side. I shall never forget the energy those hundreds of human beings put into their appeals to this unfeeling leviathan, but second after second elapsed and, keen though our observation was, it was impossible to detect the slightest deviation from her course. So far no signal of distress had been made and no instructions given. I was as yet in complete ignorance of the nature of the mishap and never asked myself how it had happened, though I could not shut my eyes to the peril we were in. However, when I asked the Abbot whether it would not be a good thing for me to go among the emigrants, he dissuaded me. "Don't go", he said. "You will only frighten them. . . . I don't think there is any danger." At that moment the *Sirio* sounded its siren. Thereupon the Abbot said, "It might be as well if you fetched our life-belts." The words were spoken in a perfectly calm tone of voice and almost smilingly. I hastened below and returned with the Abbot's life-belt—the one belonging to my own berth I could not find. On deck I found him with a group of people on their knees—one of the bishops had just imparted a general absolution. I remember placing the life-belt before my beloved Abbot, but when, a few moments later, he wished to put it on, it had somehow disappeared. "Someone has taken it", he said, with a smile, but I went and looked for another. Only some four or five minutes had elapsed since the vessel had come to a standstill. She was lying motionless on her side when I suddenly heard the rush of the mighty waters round her flanks, while the deck seemed to give way under my feet. There I was, powerless, helpless. I fell on my knees before my spiritual father for a sacramental absolution. Then he, in his turn, sank on his knees and I pronounced the words so familiar to every priest over him who had been the guardian of my childhood. "Goodbye, Fr Anscar", he said with deep emotion. I left him there and in the twinkling of an eye found myself amid a group of between two or three hundred emigrants, giving them absolution. . . . All this was only a matter of moments. Unexpected though my appearance among them was, I saw that they understood. Many eyes were raised imploringly towards heaven.

'While I was engaged in my priestly functions, all of a sudden, with lightning speed and an awful roar, more than half of the ship plunged into the depths.

'The priests whom I had left a moment ago, and hundreds of souls to whom I had given absolution as I had made my way through their ranks, vanished beneath the waves, and to the most heart-rending shrieks there succeeded the silence of death. At the same moment the mighty hulk lurched from port to starboard and was tilted at such an angle that it was impossible to maintain a vertical position. I began to slide down into the sea, when my descent was arrested by the sub-merged gunwales. By a feat of agility for which I cannot account to this day, I found myself once more on a dry part of the wreck. I could never understand how it all happened. There, then, I found a few hundred people huddled together. I took it for granted that it was only a matter of minutes before what remained of the ship would be swallowed up by the waves. So I went on with my priestly task. My fellow-travellers received absolution with perfect calm and admirable composure. "We are going to heaven, Padre; it is God's will!" Wherever I looked, a ghastly sight met my eyes, heads, legs every-where—the sea was alive. The life-boats were filling and capsizing and filling again. But what I fully expected never happened.

'As I contemplated the waters which I had come to look upon as my certain grave I saw the submerged rocks through the clear water of the Mediterranean. Then for the first time it dawned on me that we might be wedged between these rocks, and the thought flashed across my mind that after all I might see England again.

'At last, at the end of three hours' waiting, the *Joven Miguel* appeared on the scene and, having made fast to the wreck, began the work of rescue. We were three hundred souls, and it was necessary for each one to slide down into the boat with the help of a rope. The waiting must have been a real agony for most of them. As soon as I landed on the deck of the boat I became aware of the precariousness of our posi-tion, for the human load was too heavy for so small a boat, and if the monster that towered above us were to shift its position, we would be crushed by its mass. But how those good Italians peasants can pray! And how delicate their religious feelings! While we ourselves were in the jaws of death I asked them to pray for those whose dead bodies were floating around us. Their responses to my prayers and invoca-tions were made in as orderly a manner as if they had been in some quiet church in Rome or Genoa. It was a great relief when the captain of the fishing-boat himself came sliding down the rope by means of which three hundred people had made their escape from the doomed steamer. With one smart stroke of his knife he cut the cable by which his boat had been made fast to the *Sirio* and in a very few moments the waves had swept us out of the threatening shadow of the towering wreck. Life had been restored to us. It took us three-quarters of an hour to make the small bay of Palos. Darkness was falling, but the moon, then at the full, shed a silvery light upon the scene. As soon as we dropped anchor, boats came out to take us ashore in small batches. I left with the captain who had rescued us. The boat also carried the body of a woman who, I think, had died of fright. When we touched land the gallant captain took me in his arms and carried me a full ten yards so that I should not have to wade through the water. After depositing me like a small child on the dry sand, he kissed me with great affection and vanished in the night.

'Now I was literally, and bodily, taken possession of by a whole family who carried me to their home. "If Our Lady, or St Anthony, had come to visit us it would not have been a greater honour than to have a shipwrecked monk in our midst", they assured me. Half an hour later I heard a voice outside; a bishop, the speaker said, had been saved. I hastened to the house where the prelate was said to be. There I found the Archbishop of Para (Brazil). "Have you seen Fr Abbot?" I asked. "We went down in the water together and came up once more", the prelate replied. "I saw him floating on the water for about half an hour. When I last saw him he seemed to raise his hand to his forehead to make the sign of the cross."

'On the following day, at Cartagena, I met an Austrian banker whose acquaintance we had made a few hours before the catastrophe. "I heard the Abbot's voice behind me," he said, "he was praying in English." This is the last incident in the life of one who was so dear to me and whose youth and high ability held such rich promise for the Order. The bosom of the Mediterranean keeps his mortal remains to restore them glorious "when the sea shall give up the dead that are in it".'

The first inkling of the tragedy reached Buckfast in the course of the morning of 6th August. The day was the August Bank Holiday, hence the local newspaper was only delivered late in the forenoon. The big headlines announcing the wreck of the Sirio, off the Spanish coast, and the lurid and incoherent accounts of the disaster gave rise to the gravest anxiety which grew in intensity as telegrams sent in all directions failed to elicit any certain information either way. The newspaper accounts of the next day left us with little hope for the safety of our two travellers, for if both were safe, or at least one of them, we should surely have had a telegram by this time. We did not as yet fully realize Dom Anscar's calm and deliberate way of acting, or it may be that the shock to his own nervous system caused him to forget the anxiety of his brethren at home. Be this as it may, he was content to write a short note which he must have known would take several days to reach Buckfast.

Meanwhile, on the night of August 7th, a knell was rung on the Abbey's one and only bell and on the following morning the Office of the Dead was said and a Solemn Requiem sung for the Abbot and his companion. Then—when all hope had been given up, on the morning of 9th August the postman delivered a letter bearing an address in Dom Anscar's characteristic handwriting. The letter was written on the evening of the disaster and consisted of only a few lines: 'We have been shipwrecked this afternoon,' it said, 'towards three o'clock. I succeeded in saving myself to the coast of Spain. I know nothing of the fate of the Rt Rev. Fr Boniface. A Brazilian bishop who was rescued after floating in the sea for some hours tells me that he saw Fr Boniface after the accident, clinging to a plank; after about half an hour he lost sight of him.' It was typical of Abbot Anscar that he hardly ever spoke of himself—of his feelings, hopes, or disappointments. That is why, in the years that followed, he never publicly referred to his terrible ordeal on that summer's day. He may have done so for all I know in conversation with his friends, but I cannot recollect his ever having spoken of it to his community, even when the anniversary would have more than justified such reminiscences. The only exception perhaps is a letter written from Cartagena, two days after the shipwreck. 'On Sunday morning a boat belonging to the Spanish Navy took us up to Cartagena.' After a brief description of the shipwreck, he goes on: 'One must have been through all this to imagine it. . . . At one time I lost my scapular. As it is I am walking about in light slippers and I wear a borrowed hat, but I have little money. I am returning to Barcelona. . . . I can do but little here. I never thought I should have the chance of writing these few, sad lines, so certain was I of my fate. But God has judged otherwise.'

One little incident, trifling enough in itself but which the Abbot related more than once with obvious delight, may be set down by way of light relief in this tragic story. When the train that took him to Barcelona stopped at a small wayside station, an Englishman—of a military type—put his head into the compartment and asked in a loud voice, 'Does this train go to Barcelona?' Evidently foreigners were expected to understand English, and if they did not, they had only themselves to blame. On this occasion the inquiry was understood.

4

From Barcelona Dom Anscar made his way to Dourgne in France, where there are two great abbeys of our Congregation, the one of monks and the other of nuns. He made a brief stay at the convent, as appears from two letters which he wrote to the Lady Abbess shortly after his arrival at Buckfast. These letters mark the beginning of a correspondence with one not unlike those remarkable women, the great mediaeval abbesses, of whom we read in the pages of Church history.

In his first letter, written a few days after his return to Buckfast on 26th August, a Sunday, he thanks the Abbess for her kindness. 'I arrived last Sunday', he writes. 'It would be a waste of time to speak to you of the emotions that swayed my heart when I saw once more this dear and sorely-tried monastery.' He then reveals that when Abbot Natter disappeared beneath the waves he had on his finger a ring which the Abbess had given him. 'You must therefore comfort yourself with the thought that he held on to the last to this token of your friendship.' He then refers to the forthcoming election of a successor. 'I know that you will recommend this affair to Our Lord through the intercession of our beloved, saintly Fr Boniface. It is impossible to describe to you the sympathy which this calamity has won for us and the share taken in our misfortune by the non-Catholic world.' He then writes with a frankness which must surprise those who were aware of his extraordinary reserve and his unwillingness to speak of himself. True, he was not quite thirty-one, and he certainly did not think for a moment that his letters to the Abbess of Dourgne would be preserved, as they most fortunately were. 'Of all the graces which this terrible accident has brought me, I give pride of place to that of having enabled me to make your acquaintance, and to breathe, even though only for a short while, alas! the so supremely supernatural atmosphere of your little paradise. This will always remain a source of consolation for me. . . . I was fingering your beads on the boat during the short crossing on the night of Saturday to Sunday—' (He had evidently lost his rosary in the course of that other, terrible Saturday afternoon.) 'To sombre thoughts were joined memories of life and hope; one will always feel happy when working for the cause of Our Lord, if one knows that one has the support of souls so dear to His Heart.'

On 14th September 1906 the Conventual Chapter of Buckfast met for the election of a new abbot. Dom Anscar was the obvious, and practically the only candidate—had not Providence itself pointed him out to us when it preserved his precious existence in an agonizing hour?

The newly-elect was duly blessed and enthroned by the bishop of the diocese on 18th October, feast of St Luke. There is no need to describe the solemn ritual of the day for at this time such functions have not about them the spice of novelty they had fifty years ago. Nor need I quote the eloquent speeches which seasoned the repast that followed the liturgical ceremonies—all of them expressive of the high hopes that filled the hearts of the monastic family and its friends. What makes the occasion memorable is the fact that the hopes and bright anticipations so eloquently expressed were to be so magnificently fulfilled. That ever-memorable 18th October 1906 may be regarded as the end of the first period of Dom Anscar's life, a period of preparation for a providential mission. Though not quite thirty-one years old, he was ready for his noble task, for he was one of those to whom the poet's words may be fittingly applied:

> Aux âmes bien nées
> La valeur n'attend pas le nombre des années.

The nature of his own thoughts may be inferred from a letter to the Abbess of Dourgne written on 17th September, three days after his election, from the Presbytery, Ilfracombe, where he was spending the period between election and confirmation by the Abbot General: 'What is one to do in such circumstances [his election] ? One might try to persuade oneself that there is no obligation to accept, but then everybody would accuse you of obstinacy were one to persist in one's refusal, and, perhaps people would not be wrong. I don't know what your saintly Father Boniface would say, but I want to know quickly what you think, for I am told that you thought alike about many things and I shall accept your verdict as if it were his. You will have to preach to me at length and talk to me straight, for you will always have a right to look upon me as your child. . . . You might say, perhaps, that to be saved from shipwreck only to be made Superior for life is to escape from Charybdis only to be caught by Scylla, and you would assuredly not be mistaken. But since you are in the same plight, I am quite ready to believe that even a soul most dear to Our Lord might, if necessary, be caught in this net, and this thought preserves me from seeing in my position nothing but a chastisement of heaven.'

These letters were all written in French and no translation can render the exquisite delicacy of their wording. The Abbot had a wonderful mastery of the French tongue and he spoke and wrote it with perfect ease and a keen sense of the value of words. I shall have occasion to quote repeatedly from this invaluable source. One more quotation from the fourth letter to Dourgne must close this chapter: 'You put a question which it is very easy to answer. You ask whether I would accept the sandals and gloves which you were making for Abbot Boniface. So I ask! "And who has a better claim to them than I?" Knowing his affection for me and yours for him and, in him, for me, to speak for the moment only of what takes place in your heart "by concomitance". Then you ask me what souvenir I would prefer. Here is direct affection, to be sure, and no "concomitance". I think that matter is easily settled. I want to be yours from *head* to foot.' He underlines 'head' for he hints at a mitre which, as a matter of fact, the nuns made for him, and a thing of beauty it turned out to be. He goes on: 'Fr Adam Hamilton has discovered five supremely convincing reasons for my blessing to take place on 18th October, feast of St Luke. I leave it to you to discover them, but they are all based on St Luke's account of St Paul's shipwreck. If you refuse to see them you will make me credit you with the mind of a sceptic. There is only one detail that does not quite square with my situation—St Luke reached the shore with his St Paul, but I. . . .' The sentence is left unfinished.

CHAPTER VI

THE REBUILDING OF THE ABBEY CHURCH

THE last echoes of the congratulations and good wishes for a long and prosperous rule had scarcely died away when the newly-blessed Abbot, flushed with all the splendid enthusiasm of youth, made an important announcement which astonished, not to say staggered, some of the Abbey's friends and well-wishers. It was to the effect that he was resolved to enter at once upon the formidable task of rebuilding the great Abbey church upon the still extant foundations of the edifice desecrated and rifled four centuries before. For the community the announcement came as no great surprise. The project had long been 'in the air'—as a matter of fact, only too much in the air. True, in the last years of the preceding century the architect had been instructed to draw up plans and elevations of the exterior and interior of the future church, and for some years these plans and elevations—now no longer extant—were hanging on the walls of the small parlour and in the narrow corridor which led into the temporary church. By this means a vision of the future was kept alive in the mind of the community and in that of visitors and friends. However, nothing happened. At one time the late Lord Clifford approached the then Superior with a proposal to which the latter listened with eagerness akin to that with which a drowning man snatches at a straw. His Lordship's idea was that, since there was no immediate prospect of our being able to start building, at least the pillars of the future church might be erected up to the turning of the arches. An appeal was to be made to friends and benefactors to make themselves responsible for the erection of at least one pillar each, while he himself was prepared to erect all the pillars of the chancel. For the time being, no attempt would be made to raise the walls, but a small, temporary chapel would be built on the spot where the high altar of the old church had stood. A corridor—also of a temporary nature—would connect this modest structure with the south wing of the monastery, the only one so far in existence. As a matter of fact there was no thought, nor was there any pressing need, of building the east wing with its cloister, for the community was still very small.

It was fortunate that nothing came of these projects. If the plans then drawn up had been acted upon, we should now have a church of no architectural distinction, a building quite unworthy of the past and a continual disappointment for future generations. Those plans provided neither clerestory nor stone vaulting; the walls were to be plastered, and instead of a stone vaulting there would have been a so-called lean-to ceiling.

When Abbot Anscar made his announcement his financial situation was no better than that of his predecessors. However, if anything was to be done, there must be boldness amounting to rashness. Such courage, which in him was no blind instinct but a virtue born of faith and trust in God, Abbot Anscar possessed in a high degree. What was sensational in his resolve was the circumstance that since no money was available, the monks themselves—some of them at least—would be the builders in the most literal sense of the word. In our own days such an announcement would not be very surprising, but the days before the First World War were leisurely days. There were those who seemed to regard the proposal as a bad joke. Surely the thing was not practicable! For an enterprise on so large a scale you needed 'professionals' with years of practical experience behind them. But the Abbot was in deadly earnest and he met with an enthusiastic response from the community. It is related that when the plans were submitted to the local Urban District Council for their approval, one of these wise men asked, 'Do they know how to mix mortar?' There were others who also shook their heads. But in the community there was neither doubt nor hesitation, even though everybody knew that, at least for the time being, very little money was available and prospects were not particularly bright.

Having taken the momentous decision, the Abbot's first step was to organize a group of workers—a building squad—since the undertaking demanded skill no less than good will. This proved easy enough, for in the person of Brother Peter we had a most capable master-mason who had learnt his trade at Dourgne, in France. Time and again the architect, Mr Walters, declared that with Brother Peter in charge there was no need of an architect's clerk to direct the work on the spot. The actual builders were never more than six, and most of the time there were only four or five. From the very first day, up to the last also, Fr Richard—now a venerable jubilarian—worked with the Brothers. It was a constant subject of edification to see a priest at work for long hours, day after day, year in and year out, carrying out the directions of the foreman with the most perfect self-abnegation. If he was not the first on the site in the morning—he assisted regularly at the Conventual Mass—Fr Richard was invariably the last to leave. Other members of the community made their contribution to the arduous but glorious task, but it was this small group of workers who actually handled every single stone of the vast edifice.

The Abbot's contemporary letters to the Abbess of Dourgne allow us a glimpse into his mind in those early days and to follow developments almost month by month. Thus on 15th December 1906 he writes: 'In half an hour I expect the arrival of the first cartload of stone for our Abbey church which is to be erected in memory of Abbot Boniface. I have already managed to collect a certain sum and, what is more, I have a guarantee of several thousand francs annually [when writing to the Abbess he invariably translates pounds into francs], so that we can go on indefinitely. But I intend to widen the circle of our friends and subscribers. Until now I have not had time to do much, but now or never is the moment to begin, for, by reason of recent events, our monastery is the object of immense sympathy.' He then informs his correspondent that Lord Clifford had told him at once that he would build the east cloister, that is the cloister that leads into the church, as soon as a section of the sacred edifice could be used for divine service. He also mentions for the first time another great benefactress of ours, the late Lady Seaton, at this time still an Anglican. When making her first contribution, Lady Seaton promised a larger one later on, by way of making amends, as she explained, for the spoliation of which the monks of Buckland Abbey had been the victims. As the last descendant of Sir Francis Drake, the famous Elizabethan navigator, she was the owner of Buckland Abbey, which Drake had acquired in 1580. After her reception into the Church, together with her husband, Lady Seaton turned the drawing-room of the house— originally the chancel of the Abbey church—into an oratory, placing the altar on the very spot where the high altar had stood previous to the spoliation. Thus it came about that during the remainder of that noble lady's lifetime, Mass was frequently offered within the walls of the mansion that had been an Abbey church for centuries. Abbot Anscar had taken the Abbess into his confidence before his public announcement, for five days after his blessing he had written: 'Now I am going to talk to you about the little monument which I hope to raise to the memory of your Saint [viz. Abbot Natter], namely, the transept of the old Abbey church. You will smile—but you know very well that I am only thirty [*sic*]. In another thirty years' time I shall not be so very old, and during all that time I shall apply myself to this task without ceasing, and should the need arise, I shall beg for a stone even from you. Given time and patience one might construct a world. I do not expect donations of large sums but shall look for small but regular contributions—and I shall know how to wait. Yesterday I spoke of my plan for the first time and on the spot I was handed one pound sterling. It is a beginning.'

Abbot Anscar was a great admirer and a keen reader—at least in his early years as a monk—of the works of St Teresa of Avila. His thoughts at this stage of the enterprise were probably those to which that wonderful woman gave expression at a moment when she was setting out for one of her many foundations, with no resources except five *duros*: 'Five *duros* and Teresa is not much,' she said, 'but five *duros*, Teresa and God is everything.'

In a letter of 19th December of the same year he informs the Abbess that, at the time of writing, the architect's plans were not yet to hand, but all was ready for a start. In any case he was determined that building operations should begin 'in this year of destiny, 1906'. In point of fact, preparations for the momentous event had been going on for years—one might say from the time of the monks' return and the day when a lucky sounding of the ground with a crow-bar revealed the existence of foundations, several feet below the surface. For years, during the hour which everyone had to devote to some manual task, one of the most regular jobs had been the uncovering of these ancient walls. The first step towards the actual reconstruction had been made possible by the generosity of the Dowager Lady Clifford, who in her will left a sum of money for this purpose. This was in the last decade of the last century. As there was no prospect of any large-scale building operations, the money was spent in repairing the old foundations and concreting them over, up to the level of the soil. As a result of these providential preparations, our Brothers were able to start work on the actual walls on the very first day.

The capital in hand on that day was exceedingly small. But so is the acorn when it drops to the ground; but let it but sink into the soil and it grows into a mighty oak. One of our assets was a horse—a fine, handsome mare, once one of Lord Clifford's hunters, but now somewhat reduced in rank when, instead of galloping after the fox, she was made to take her place between the shafts of our ancient farm cart or, on special occasions, when some important personage had to be met at, or taken to, the railway station, between those of our humble wagonette. Our good, genial neighbour, the late Mr John Beard, of Northwood Farm, who seemed to regard the Abbey and its inmates as but an extension of his own lovely farmland and his delightful family, put at our disposal a valuable sand-pit in his stretch of the river-bank. The beautiful, clean sand is carried down from the heights of Dartmoor by the river when in spate, a frequent occurrence in this climate. But the best and most assured resource was the Abbot's and the community's trust in God and—last but by no means least—their reliance on the well-tested generosity of the public. Needless to add that this twofold trust was never frustrated.

The Vigil of the Epiphany, 5th January 1907, will always be a *dies memorabilis* in the annals of Buckfast. On that wintry morning, at the conclusion of the Conventual Mass and the Office of Sext, the whole community, followed by a small group of friends from the village, went in procession to the site of the new church. When all had taken their places at the north-east corner of the foundations, that is roughly in the space between the Chapel of the Blessed Sacrament and the transept of the present church, the *Veni Creator* was sung. After the Abbot had said a few appropriate prayers he duly laid the first stone, under which he had placed three medals, viz. of Our Lady, of St Benedict and of the reigning Pope, St Pius X. This stone, of course, was not the actual foundation-stone which is embodied in the great pillar on the epistle side of the high altar, but simply one of the thousands of dressed limestones of which the church is built. The Antiphon *Sub tuum praesidium* was then sung, and the simple but impressive ceremony ended with the singing of the heart-stirring strophes of the Hymn of Our Lady of Buckfast:

> Thy shrine stood here, full in the golden noontide
> Of light then all unveiled . . .
> The dark was long, but now the star of morning
> Has risen through the night. . . .

A keen, cutting north wind was blowing down from the snow-powdered Dartmoor hills, but all hearts were aglow, and even the youngest boy in the alumnate could not fail to realize that this was indeed a solemn hour in the life of the community—had we not put our hand to a tremendous but glorious task, the end of which none could foresee? In a way that no one could have anticipated, we were making history, or if that is too grandiose a phrase, we were setting a precedent, for that which Buckfast undertook on that wintry morning has been imitated and repeated many times over in other parts of the country.

In a letter of 26th January the Abbot was able to inform the Abbess of Dourgne that a sizable stretch of wall was already showing. He also tells her that the capital in hand amounted to ten thousand francs, and adds, 'Since we do the work ourselves, we can go forward with full confidence.' As a matter of fact, such had been the progress of the work that early in the same year preparations were made for the formal, liturgical laying of the foundation-stone of the new church by the Bishop of Plymouth. The date fixed for this joyful occasion was 2nd July, the feast of the Visitation. The choice of the date was prompted, in the first instance, by the fact that the new house of God was to be dedicated to the Blessed Virgin Mary. A further reason for the choice of this feast was that it was on that day, in the year 1850, that Père Muard had inaugurated the monastic life at La Pierre-qui-Vire, which, as we have seen in a previous chapter, was the spiritual parent of the community of Buckfast.

This function was the first of a fairly long sequence of festive occasions when large crowds gathered from all parts of Devon and beyond. Abbot Anscar had made no secret of what was afoot at Buckfast. Though the start was quiet enough, it was not long before our building activities attracted public attention, and it was obvious that the Abbot was far from averse to any amount of publicity. He welcomed it, for the success of his undertaking depended on it. On this occasion he left nothing undone in order to draw as large a crowd as possible. To this end he secured the presence of a preacher whose name was a household word at that time. To the present generation Fr Bernard Vaughan is little more than a name—if so be that it has heard of him at all; but half a century ago this Jesuit priest was one of the most popular clerical figures in the country and he enjoyed a great reputation as a preacher with non-Catholics as well as with Catholics. His reputation was chiefly based on a series of sermons preached at Farm Street during the London season, on 'The Sins of Society'. As a member of an ancient Catholic family which, in that very period, gave to the Church a number of priests and bishops and one cardinal—not to mention several religious and nuns—blessed with a magnificent physical presence, a splendid, musical voice, a vivid imagination, a warm and lively temperament, and a keen sense, not to say love, of the dramatic, Fr Vaughan, so the Abbot thought, was sure to prove a powerful attraction. Nor was he mistaken. The congregation that afternoon cannot have been short of two thousand people—a remarkable figure, for in those days the motor-car was in its growing pains and liable to the ills and ailments of infancy, coaches and buses were unknown, and Buckfastleigh—and Buckfast—were only served by a single-track line of the Great Western Railway, the station itself being a good mile and a half from the Abbey.

The splendid liturgical pageant was preceded by pontifical Vespers in the crowded temporary church. A stately procession of monks, diocesan clergy and people then made its way to the site of the future church, preceded by the Buckfastleigh town band, whose harmonies subsequently supported and reinforced the singing of the hymn with which the ceremony ended.

The preacher was expected to speak from a platform on which the bishop of the diocese and his assistants had taken their places, but this arrangement seemed much too commonplace for an enterprising person like Fr Bernard Vaughan. Boldly, therefore, though cautiously, the preacher climbed onto the pillar on which the foundation-stone was to be laid and there took a somewhat precarious stand. His daring led to an unrehearsed incident which might have had serious consequences. There came a moment when the orator, forgetting that he stood unprotected against his own impetuous movements and gestures, instinctively sought some kind of support. He grasped the loose chain of the pulley by which the heavy foundation-stone was to be hoisted into position, but as he did so, there being no counter-weight, the chain came down with a loud, grating sound. The preacher, though he made a profound if involuntary bow to the congregation, did not lose his presence of mind, and with remarkable agility for one no longer young, and of somewhat portly figure, managed to regain his balance while the audience heaved an almost audible sigh of relief.

As for the sermon itself, one may safely say at this day that its success was perhaps due to the personality of the preacher rather than to its intrinsic merit—for one thing, the preacher touched on too many topics. He spoke of Our Lady, of St Peter, of the Pope, of England and King Edward 'the Peacemaker', and finally of the work in hand. He made an earnest appeal to his hearers to show their interest in the monks' undertaking in a practical way, all the more so as 'the work

was to be wholly carried out by monkish [sic] hands', and the sacred
edifice would be 'a spiritual fortress for the safety of this country'.

This solemn day was followed by a long series of silent, uneventful
months and years during which the building grew slowly but steadily.
The Abbot had wisely planned to carry out the huge task in two stages.
The total length of the building is 240 feet. He decided to complete
only the most important portion, which was also the most expensive,
viz. the chancel, the transepts with their two chapels, two bays of the
nave and the ambulatory behind the high altar with its six chapels.
The central tower, resting on four massive piers, was to be carried
to a height sufficient to accommodate a peal of bells promised by one
of our oldest non-Catholic friends, the late Sir Robert Harvey of
Dundridge, near Totnes, who had been knighted by King Edward VII
a few years before this date. This honour from his sovereign gave that
upright, forthright, plain-spoken man immense satisfaction while it
did not in the least diminish his natural simplicity. If some old-school-
tie prig chanced to ask him, 'Oh! Sir Robert, what school were you
at?' he would reply, 'The school of adversity.' In point of fact, he
had done remarkably well in that school. He had very considerable
business interests in South America, and his wife was a South American
and, of course, a Catholic. For her benefit, Sir Robert built a large and
beautiful chapel as an annexe to his house. Its inauguration was a considerable event. Bishop Graham pontificated, Fr Adam Hamilton
preached, and monks from Buckfast formed the choir.

Sir Robert was a shrewd businessman, but he was also a staunch
Christian, with a strong, sincerely held faith. His faith and trust in the
power of prayer, and, I may add, the prayers of the monks of Buckfast in particular—'my friends the monks of Buckfast' he used to say—
was quite remarkable. All his benefactions, and they were many, were
so many thanksgivings for blessings received, as he put it and, we may
be sure, sincerely believed, through the monks' prayers. His munificent
gift of a peal of bells was one such acknowledgment. It was also
intended as a memorial to Lady Alida Harvey, whose death dealt him
a blow from which he never recovered, for under a bluff exterior, Sir
Robert had a very sensitive and affectionate nature. To Dom Adam
Hamilton, with whom he was on particularly intimate terms, he sometimes confided the secret of his loneliness; but when that most genial
of old monks suggested he should look for someone to take her place,
he only shook his head and said, 'No! I could never hope to find another
treasure like her.' There was, in that seemingly hard-boiled man of

affairs, a strong sentimental, not to say romantic strain. But, as I have said, he was a sincere Christian, a lover of the Bible and, what is getting so rare in these days, a regular reader of the sacred volume. I still have a vivid recollection of a visit to Dundridge with the Abbot. When we got back to the drawing-room after lunch, Sir Robert, who regarded the Abbot as a man possessed of unlimited erudition, requested him to explain to him verses seventeen and eighteen of the second chapter of St Matthew's gospel. Sir Robert was puzzled by the reference to Rachel. Actually he was by no means the first to wonder what connexion there was between Rachel's grief and the slaughter of the Innocents and the mourning of their mothers.

Napoleon is said to have loved church bells, and when he set out for St Helena, he is reported to have said that one of the things he would miss most was the sound of church bells. This may or may not be an authentic saying—what is certain is that Sir Robert loved the sound of church bells. He was determined that when the tower of the new church would at last raise its head to the sky, the Dartmoor breezes should waft the music of bells far and wide. Early in 1910 he presented Fr Abbot with a cheque for £1,000. The latter, with the donor's enthusiastic approval, decided not to invest the money, as had been intended at first, but to order the peal of bells at once. For the time being they would be hung on top of the 'Abbot's Tower.' In this way the donor would have the satisfaction of hearing his bells while their unsatisfactory location would stimulate work on the church and tower. The liturgical blessing of the bells—their 'baptism' in the popular speech of Catholic countries—was another spectacular event in the story of the restoration of the Abbey.

At the time of the suppression of the Abbey in 1539 there were five bells in the church tower. The buildings were dismantled, the lead stripped from the roofs, and the bells bought by the men of Buckfastleigh for the sum of thirty-three pounds and fifteen shillings, for the parish church. This sum went into the pocket of Sir Thomas Denys, the new owner of the place. In an inventory of Church property made in 1553 we find this entry: 'Buckfastleigh: lllj belles in the Church, j belle in the comenhouse and lj belles in the chapell there.' These bells have been recast on three occasions, viz. in 1712, 1749, and 1933, when two bells were added to the previous peal of six.[1]

While they were in the 'Abbot's Tower' the bells could only be

---

[1] Cf. *Transactions of the Devonshire Association*, Vol. LXVIII, pp. 215-20.

chimed. They were rung for the first time on Christmas Eve 1920, for by that time the first section of the central tower—what is now the ringing chamber—had been completed. There they remained for another thirteen years, when they were taken down and recast by the well-known firm of Messrs. Taylor & Co., of Loughborough, but this time the weight of the peal was considerably increased and a magnificent *bourdon*, christened *Hosanna*, was added to it. This seven and a half ton bell was one of the many munificent gifts of Miss Hilda de Trafford.

To complete the story of the bells I may anticipate a little so as not to have to revert to the subject. It was obvious that so splendid a peal could not remain for ever in its first location, were it only for the fact that the ringing had to be done from the narrow gallery in the lantern of the tower, fifty-one feet above the floor of the church. This procedure was not without an element of risk, and at least on one occasion one of the ringers had a narrow escape from grave danger when he was swept off his feet and swung towards the ceiling by the downward momentum of the bell, the rope of which he had failed to let go in time. For some time there was a good deal of discussion about the height of the tower. One school of thought urged that an unduly lofty tower would dwarf the church, while another favoured a tall one. In the end it was decided to build into the sky, to a height, in fact, of 156 feet. The tower was only completed in 1938—six years after the consecration of the church. This was the crowning event of the long years of steady, patient toil, since that cold January day in 1907, when building operations began, and 2nd July of the same year, when the foundation-stone was laid—roughly a period of thirty years. The bells however, had been hung in their permanent home two years before the completion of the tower.

CHAPTER VII

THE WAR YEARS: 1914–1918

WE must now for a while take our eyes off the pleasing spectacle of the peaceful activities that filled the first seven years of Dom Anscar's rule as Abbot of Buckfast and at the same time call up from an already distant past the memory of the fears and alarums of four long years of war. On Sunday, 2nd August 1914, Germany invaded Belgium, whose neutrality she had pledged herself to respect and, if need be, even to defend. It became evident at once that England could not be content with a mere diplomatic protest; nor could she idly stand aside and watch France, her next-door neighbour and associate in an *entente cordiale*, being beaten to the ground by her powerful enemy. War with Germany was unavoidable if England's honour was to be saved. War was declared on 4th August, an ominous date in Abbot Anscar's life and in the history of Buckfast, for only eight years had gone by since the tragedy which robbed the Abbey of its first abbot on the afternoon of that same August day.

It cannot be my purpose to dwell at length on the memory of those tragic years which put an end to a long period of unparalleled prosperity for this country and which proved to be the starting-point of a blood-less revolution which issued in a new social order, except in so far as their impact affected the subject of this story and the religious family of which he was the much-loved head. For an outsider the very composition of that family may be said to have constituted a formidable problem, seeing that the majority of its members were German-born, hence 'enemy aliens' in the official terminology. True, there were three Frenchmen, and the Abbot and one other priest had become naturalized British subjects some years before that fateful date, but the fact remained that the monks constituted a large foreign group in this peaceful countryside. It had never occurred to anyone that it would be a good and seemly thing for all the professed religious to seek British citizenship, since by the very fact of their monastic profession they were permanently settled in the country of their adoption, in which they enjoyed privileges their native land denied them. It may

be argued that it seemed utterly impossible—at least to ordinary people
—that there should ever be war between two nations that had so much
in common, in spite of the provocative and bombastic speeches and
hasty actions of Germany's blustering ruler. After all, was not the
Kaiser a grandson of Queen Victoria? and is not blood thicker than
water? Moreover, up to that time, every crisis had somehow ended
without bloodshed, if not without resentment and real anxiety in the
minds of those who kept a watchful and anxious eye on the political
barometer.

But now war was a hard fact, and the shock and bewilderment were
all the greater as a long period of peace—at least in Europe—had left
this nation unprepared for such an emergency. Up to 1914 England's
wars had been fought in distant lands. Now war was on our doorstep,
and in spite of airy prophecies of a speedy victorious termination of the
conflict, since Germany found herself between two fires, even the
unthinking realized before many weeks were over that the struggle
would be fierce and protracted.

What would be the fate of a community most of whose members
were natives of a country with whom England was about to be locked
in a life-and-death struggle? I think it is no disparagement of any
nation if I set down what I have always felt, viz. that what actually
happened would have been impossible anywhere else, least of all in
Germany—not to speak of France. It is no reflection on other countries
if one states the plain fact that during those sombre years the community of Buckfast was treated with a consideration, a kindliness and
generosity of which only a truly magnanimous people was capable in
circumstances well calculated to call forth very different sentiments.
Not that there never was any hostility. It would have been absurd not
to expect it, or to be surprised at it at such a time, but it remains as a
splendid memory that the public authorities, that is, the men ultimately responsible for the safety of the country, at no time allowed
themselves to be swept off their feet even by protracted and acri-
monious agitation. Firmly, after a careful study of the circumstances,
they came to the humane conclusion that the community of Buckfast
was not to be disturbed, and from this decision they never swerved, for
it had been arrived at after a calm, serene and judicious weighing of
the various arguments brought forward by the handful of persons who
thought that here was a chance of restricting, if not of wholly destroy-
ing, the religious influence of the Abbey. The only restriction that was
ever placed upon the monks was that they were not to step beyond the

ABBOT VONIER WITH BISHOP GRAHAM OF PLYMOUTH ON THE DAY OF
HIS ABBATIAL BLESSING, 18TH OCTOBER 1906

[*facing p. 54*

THE SITE OF BUCKFAST ABBEY CHURCH IN THE AUTUMN OF 1906

THE SAME SITE IN THE AUTUMN OF 1907

boundaries of the Abbey grounds. This was no great hardship; in fact the monks were even permitted to go into a large field adjoining our grounds but belonging to our good neighbour, Mr Beard. It may even be said that the long-drawn agony of the war years proved a providential opportunity for a fuller realization of the monastic ideal, the basic element of which consists precisely in that a monk withdraws from the interests and pursuits of the world so as to be free to devote all his powers to the immediate service of God.

The anxiety of the early days of the war was increased by the unfortunate circumstance that Abbot Anscar was not with his community. Of late his health had deteriorated considerably and his medical adviser had urged a cure abroad. The Abbot had left Buckfast about the middle of July for Bad Gastein, in Austria. His arrival in that well-known resort almost synchronized with Austria's declaration of war against Serbia, as a sequel to the brutal assassination in the streets of Serajevo of Archduke Ferdinand and his consort. Those of us who lived through those feverish days cannot have forgotten the dismay this step caused in every European country. The hideous spectre of war—European war—cast its baneful shadow upon those sunny midsummer days, but like many others, the Abbot no doubt imagined that the fire thus kindled would not become a general conflagration. Before many days the difference between peace and war was to be brought home to him in no uncertain fashion. At a later date, in *The Tablet* of 23rd January 1915, he gave a personal account of what befell him at this time.

Meanwhile, in our own neighbourhood, the most fantastic rumours began to circulate as soon as some of the local folk became aware of the fact that the Abbot had gone abroad some time before the outbreak of war. Gastein is situate amid magnificent mountain scenery. A short time after his arrival Dom Anscar set out for a walk in the direction of the mountains, the valleys between which are linked by the imposing viaducts of the Tauern Railway, which were being guarded by soldiers. 'Word went round immediately', the Abbot wrote, 'that a dangerous individual was roaming about in the neighbourhood of the all-important viaducts. It was rumoured that I was a Serbian spy! Rain had fallen most of the day and evening came early. Before long, in the gathering gloom, a soldier fancied he had perceived the Serbian spy behind a tree. He fired at once. Meanwhile I had gone back to the hotel. There was some firing during the night, but no dead body could be found. When morning came a search was made in the town, when the police eventually discovered my whereabouts. For the moment the affair ended with mutual apologies, but from this moment I was suspect and on the day on which a state of war was declared between Austria and England I was arrested in the market-place of Gastein, as a British subject, though with no end of apologies on the part of my captors. That same night I was taken to Salzburg under an armed escort, and there, on the Sunday morning, my case was gone into by the military. Meanwhile I was left pacing the length of the platform of the railway station, between two soldiers with fixed bayonets. At the end of a two hours' enquiry the authorities came to tell me they were sorry for what had happened. They requested me to go to a hotel of my own choice. "Oh!" I said, "I see it is impossible for me to leave Austria, as I am a British subject. With your permission I shall choose the interesting Abbey of St Peter for my hotel during the term of my internment.'" Needless to say, the 'prisoner' was most hospitably received by his Benedictine brethren of this famous abbey, the oldest, or one of the two or three oldest abbeys north of the Alps. Steps were taken at once to secure his release. They proved successful, and by the middle of October, thanks to the intervention of the Abbot Primate with the Austrian ambassador to the Vatican, and the latter's representations at Vienna, he was given a safe-conduct for neutral Switzerland. 'I must say', the Abbot stated, 'that during the time of my detention I met with the greatest kindness and courtesy everywhere; thus, for instance, the soldiers who guarded me would come up to me, when relieved, to tell me how very sorry they were for their part in the business; they protested that they too were good Catholics.'

Great was the community's joy when on 15th October, St Teresa's day, a telegram announced the Abbot's arrival. The day turned out to be one of those genial, mellow autumn days of golden sunshine such as we often enjoy in the sweet West Country. The mere presence of Fr Abbot was a comfort and a reassurance. His return came none too soon, for shortly afterwards there was a sudden alarm when an order was issued by Whitehall for the immediate arrest and internment of all German subjects. Fr Abbot hastened to London to see an old friend of his and of the Abbey. This was none other than one of the men who would be responsible for the execution of the order, Sir Basil Thomson. Sir Basil had come to know both the Abbot and several of the monks of Buckfast during his term of office as Governor of Dartmoor Prison. For many years we had supplied for the Catholic prison chaplain during his annual leave and on other occasions. Sir

Basil had come to know Buckfast well. When the Abbot explained the situation to him, orders were promptly given that the German monks were not to be interfered with.

In spite of the war the Abbot's extra-mural activities suffered scarcely any interruption. Thus he was to preach a course of sermons at Westminster Cathedral during the month of January 1915. This was all the more remarkable as the first Sunday of the new year had been set apart as a national day of prayer for the victory of the allied armies. Fr Abbot hesitated at first, but the administrator of the cathedral, the late Mgr Howlett, pressed him to accept on the ground that his appearance in its pulpit would be particularly appropriate on that Sunday! Fr Maturin, the well-known convert and notable preacher, who was to be one of the 1,500 victims of the inhuman attack on the *Lusitania*, and who was at this time in charge of the Catholic undergraduates at Oxford, invited the Abbot to give another course of Sunday conferences to his by now sadly depleted flock. I think it is safe to say that it was these conferences, and the valuable and interesting contacts for which they provided the occasion, that inspired the Abbot with the great love he cherished for Oxford. As a matter of fact, even while the Abbey church was as yet unfinished, he was actively studying the possibility of founding a Benedictine monastery, not in the city itself, but within easy reach of it, in which the liturgy of the Catholic Church would be carried out in all its beauty. He was profoundly convinced—and who would say him nay?—that the 'Work of God', carried out to perfection, would be the most attractive as well as the most persuasive form of apostolate. Such a monastery, he thought, would meet a real need. The undergraduates—and their elders—would have before their eyes an object-lesson that would not be lost on men of whom not a few were at the University not merely for the purpose of securing a degree, but for the sake of the human culture of which Oxford is both the symbol and the generous dispenser. One of the disappointments of his career was the failure of his plans to that end when success was almost in sight.

These varied engagements, which were so many marks of confidence and proofs of esteem from men whose good opinion was most worth having, were calculated to comfort the Abbot's spirit in the course of the strong and protracted effort that was about to be made, not merely to get the monks confined within the monastic enclosure, but to have them removed to a concentration camp. The tale is a painful one, but since most, if not all, the people who were then ranged against the Abbey are no longer alive, it can be no breach of Christian charity to recall those distressing events, all the more so as the final issue of the struggle was yet another proof of our Lady's tender care and powerful protection of those who honour her on this spot, hallowed by so many centuries of prayer and praise.

On 7th May 1915, the German navy perpetrated a deed of particularly revolting cruelty when, without warning, one of its submarines torpedoed the Cunarder *Lusitania* and so caused the death of some 1,500 civilians—one of them being Fr Abbot's friend, Fr Maturin. This outrage caused public anger and indignation to flare up to a dangerous degree. Scenes of violence against Germans occurred in London and other cities. To meet the public demand for action, the government ordered the immediate arrest of all German males between the ages of fifteen and fifty-five; yet even then the authorities were willing to consider applications for exemptions from this order. Exemption was at once granted to the German members of this community, but hostile agitation by the Urban District Council of Buckfastleigh and in the local press continued for several months.

In October—actually on the Saturday before Rosary Sunday—a special commission came from London for the purpose of studying the whole question on the spot. Its members first met the Urban District Council and afterwards came to the Abbey. After visiting the house they asked to see all the aliens, but they stated from the first that whatever might have to be done, the priests would not be interfered with. These gentlemen could not have been more courteous or considerate. The upshot of the long-drawn campaign was that the 'enemy aliens' would have to remain within the boundaries of the monastic enclosure for the duration of the war.

It may be of some interest, in retrospect, to quote a specimen of the kind of letter that occasionally appeared in the local press. In a letter, signed *Pro bono publico*—we all know the type—the writer claimed that a statement to the effect that 'the Kaiser has promised not only temporal power to the Pope if he is successful in this war, but that . . . with the Sultan's help he shall have Jerusalem, with sufficient territory to support a cardinal-viceroy in Palestine', had never been denied. The writer then proceeds: 'This might go far to explain much that has been strange in the conduct of the Pope during this war. It would make it doubly dangerous to have German monks at large in our midst at this time owing fealty to both Pope and Kaiser.' Comment would seem superfluous, but in point of fact not a few of the 'enemy aliens', particularly the lay brothers, were without nationality, they having formally renounced German nationality by a legal transaction, with a view to avoiding the possibility of being called up for military service. However, none had been naturalized—not that they were unwilling, but the stringent poverty of the house could not easily afford the very considerable expenditure.

On the other hand, the writer of another letter, addressed to an evening paper, declined to hide his identity but signed with his full name, though he knew quite well that he was courting unpopularity with *Pro bono publico* and his ilk. The letter honours the writer while to the monks it came as a ray of sunshine, hence it must be quoted in full: 'In your issue of last night you say that "the interests of the Kingdom demand that all enemy aliens at Buckfast Abbey should be removed". If all enemy aliens in this country (including eminent and powerful financiers, only naturalized since the war began, and with sons fighting in that army whose atrocities in Belgium and elsewhere have caused the name of Germany to stink throughout the civilized world) were safely interned, I know of no reason why the monks of Buckfast should be exempted from so salutary a precaution. But let me quote a paragraph from a letter in yesterday's *Daily Mail* over the well-known signature of William Le Queux: [1] "according to Sir John Simon's statement, 7,233 enemy aliens have been granted certificates exempting them from internment, while there are in the London area no fewer than 9,555 male and 8,207 female enemy aliens, with 147 others living happily in the confines of Bradford, while 471 males of the same genus are actually allowed by our paternal government to reside in prohibited areas."

'While the country can swallow this very multitudinous camel, surely it need not strain at the tiny gnat of some few monks at Buckfast, where their continuance is conditional on their not leaving it, and where they are nobly occupied in raising to the glory of God and their own eternal honour a reproduction of the building of their Order upon foundations which have lain for centuries beneath the sod".'

The letter bears the signature of John Edward Moss. Sir John knew the Abbot and the monks; in the sequel also he showed himself a loyal and staunch friend of our Abbey.

Another letter from one of the leading personalities at Ashburton, the late Mr. Ralph Firth of Place, Ashburton, must be preserved from

[1] William Le Queux was a neighbour of ours for a number of years, when he rented Hawson Court—an ancient possession of the Abbey, presented to 'St Mary of Buckfast and the monks serving God there', by Sir Robert de Helion, about the middle of the thirteenth century.

oblivion. It is in itself a tribute to the noble character of the writer, while it gave Abbot Anscar and the community both comfort and encouragement. Mr Firth was a deeply religious man, not a Catholic, but, as the letter shows, full of understanding of what the Abbey stands for.

'*Place, Ashburton, 13th February* 1916.

'MY LORD ABBOT,

I am addressing you because I wish to express my sympathy with your community in the trouble you have from the attacks now being made on you. I should have nothing to say if I could believe that these attacks were really prompted by love of country—as is pretended. It is perfectly reasonable for people to suspect men belonging to an enemy country—especially when nerves are upset in the middle of a great war. That would be natural and only to be expected, though in the case of your community we who live in this part of Devonshire have little reason to share such feelings. But I do not believe that such suspicions have very much to do with the present agitation—and it is because I feel that the opportunity has simply been used to arouse once more intolerance in religious questions, that I venture to write to you to say how very greatly I regret it. I believe that there are very many who share my view exactly. As you are very well aware, there is an extreme but ever dwindling party bitterly opposed to your religion, though strangely tolerant of all others. The present occasion serves them in enabling them to make themselves heard once more. Assuredly it will pass.

Believe me yours very faithfully,

RALPH FIRTH.'

In a P.S. he says: 'I am afraid that newspaper controversy only adds heat to the quarrel and gives importance to what is negligible.'

On New Year's Day 1917, our good friend Sir Robert Harvey wrote: 'My wishes for your welfare, tranquillity, and peace of mind are equally strong, in which I enclose the whole of your community. I hope this year will terminate your troubles and that we may all live in Christian and fraternal love, and that blessed peace will again smile on our land.

As soon as I can save some petrol, I will visit you. . . . Pray ever for my dear boys in their dangerous occupations. They are well now, for which I devoutly thank God.

Assuring you of my unaltered friendship and esteem,

I am your always sincerely,

ROB. HARVEY.'

Nearly two years were to elapse before these prayers were answered, but by then the agitation had spent most of its energy and, as will appear from a document presently to be quoted, the end of the war found the entire community engaged in its normal pursuits and thankful to God and to our Lady whose mighty hand had sheltered and guarded it.

It was necessary to describe at least summarily the anxieties of those critical years, were it only to pay tribute to the kindness of friends, the wisdom of the Abbot, and above all to the magnanimity and serene sense of justice displayed by the men who were responsible for the safety of the realm in those perilous days, and who refused to behave otherwise than with the most exquisite courtesy and consideration for this community. Their names, and the memory of what they did for it, will assuredly remain alive as long as there are monks at Buckfast.

It will be useful to give here a translation of a memorandum, written in French, in which the Abbot, at the request of the Abbot General in Rome, summed up the story of those years. It is entitled *Buckfast Abbey from* 1914 *to* 1918:

'The history of a monastery in the years 1914–1918 must necessarily be an account of the way in which a community passed through the terrible crisis of a world war. This is particularly true of our Abbey of Buckfast. When England entered into the war against Germany, two-thirds of the community of Buckfast consisted of German subjects, most of them—priests, clerics, novices, lay brothers—of military age, not to mention some alumni who reached that age during the course of the war. The outstanding fact, which our community will always keep in grateful remembrance, is that of its complete preservation, without any loss whatsoever. When hostilities ended in 1918, the life of the community was what it had been in July 1914, before the catastrophe. At the end of the long-drawn trial the Abbot was able to say: *Quos dedisti mihi custodivi, et nemo ex eis periit* (Jo. xvii. 12).

'Nevertheless, the first phase of the war period was not reassuring. At the outbreak of war the Abbot was in Austria. As a British subject he was arrested on 15th August 1914 and ordered to remain at Salzburg for the duration of hostilities. The hospitality extended to him by the Abbot of St Peter of Salzburg, Dom Willibald Halthauer, was a great consolation for the prisoner, but the latter's supreme desire was to return to Buckfast, there to share the fortunes of his community. Thanks to the efficacious intervention of the Abbot Primate, Dom Fidelis von Stotzingen, the Austrian government authorized him to set out for England. Leaving Salzburg on 6th October 1914, he travelled without difficulty via Switzerland and France, and returned to his monastery in England on the 15th of the same month. He found the whole community living a peaceful existence. However, difficulties and dangers were beginning to take shape. The Abbot was no sooner home than he had to meet a peril which never ceased to threaten the community right up to the end of the war. In October 1914 the cry was first heard which was to be raised again and again with ever-growing insistence, demanding that all strangers of enemy nationality should be sent to internment camps. Such a measure would have been the ruin of our community. Fortunately, during the years of peace we had won reliable and influential friends who loyally stood by us during the war years. When the popular cry arose, demanding the internment of "enemy aliens", the Abbot hastened to London and, through the intervention of an important personage, was able to prevent the execution of this measure, at the very moment when it was about to be applied to this community.

'As the war went on, the situation became increasingly acute, but the British government continued to protect us. In 1916 those members of the community who were subjects of the enemy powers were ordered not to leave the boundaries of the Abbey property. This order was strictly enforced up to 8th September 1919, but the government would not permit any other interference with the life of the community, notwithstanding the clamour of certain circles hostile to the Catholic Church. On 7th October 1917 an important government commission came for the purpose of studying on the spot the position of those monks who were "enemy aliens". The result of this visit was completely favourable to the monks.[1] In the course of those long years of enforced inactivity outside, the interior life of the community grew stronger, and that without any hindrance. The community never suffered any serious privations; the building of the church made great strides during those years of destruction; our English friends continued to help us in this great task as if everything were for the best in the best

[1] Ten years later, on 10th September 1927, the late Sir Louis Dane, who had headed the Home Office Commission, paid a friendly visit to Buckfast. He was greatly amused to find a policeman at the entrance to the Abbey grounds, whose duty it was not to 'invigilate' the monks but to regulate the movement of cars and coaches which were bringing large numbers of visitors to the Abbey. In the course of his conversation with the Abbot he said that what finished the U.D.C.'s agitation was their refusal to provide guards for the monks. 'What they wanted was "to hoof them out" [sic], patriotism had nothing to do with it.' *Sunt lacrymae rerum*, says the poet, but there is also an irony in the course of human events.

of worlds. The French and English members of the community assisted their German brethren in every way they could during these years of enforced restrictions. Two of our French priests were called to serve their country, but when on leave from the theatre of war they returned to the monastery and mixed with their brethren as usual.

'At last, in 1919, the peace treaties were signed, and in September of that same year, on the feast of our Lady's Nativity, the Abbot was officially informed that full liberty of movement was restored to all the members of the community without exception. When the monks appeared for the first time outside the enclosure they were the objects of a joyous ovation on the part of the people. The community is conscious that it was a special dispensation of divine Providence that enabled it to continue its normal life without a single day's interruption, and this at a time when, according to human previsions, its very existence was extremely problematic.

Signed: DOM ANSCAR VONIER.

Abbot of Buckfast.'

To Dourgne the Abbot wrote on 9th August 1919: 'More than ever we need the help of the powerful Maiden, the *Virgo potens*. The world's upheaval drives us into the arms of her who is essentially *plenitudo pacis*. The "powerful Virgin" has protected us in spite of everything . . . but it is evident that the official Peace will mark the opening of a new chapter in the history of our monastery.'

Prophetic words! Humanly speaking, the immediate future looked dim enough, yet contrary to expectation, not only was there no lack of vocations, but, on the contrary, a great many young men—all natives of the country—sought admission to the community, now doubly before the public eye by reason of the restoration of the ancient Abbey church and as a result of the notoriety involuntarily acquired through the activities of a handful of noisy people who, perhaps unconsciously, sought to bring about the ruin of the community.

CHAPTER VIII

THE OPENING OF THE ABBEY CHURCH IN 1922

*Elegi et sanctificavi locum istum, ut sit nomen meum ibi in
sempiternum.* —2 Paralip. vii. 16.

ALL through the years of the organized, scientific destruction of men
and things that we call war, work on the Abbey church went on from
day to day, though progress was slowed down by the shortage of stone,
cement and the hundred and one requisites for an undertaking of such
magnitude—not to speak of the lack of funds. Those were anxious
days, and but for the admirable and most self-sacrificing generosity of
a benefactress whose name I am not at liberty to divulge, the work
would of necessity have come to a standstill. For many months the
Abbot—as a builder—lived 'from hand to mouth', but month after
month the above-mentioned lady would provide him with enough
money to carry on during the next phases of the moon. Again and
again I heard the Abbot say: 'I went to call on —— and we can carry
on for another month.'

With the return of peace and the relaxation of the control of building
materials, the pace was greatly accelerated and funds began to come in
in a steady and increasing flow; so much so indeed that by the end of
1921 it became possible to fix a date for the opening of the section of
the vast edifice on which the Brothers had been working ever since
that chilly January day in 1907 on which the first row of stones had
been laid upon the ancient foundations—that is, roughly two-thirds
of the sacred edifice.

The announcement was made in the pages of *Chimes*, the modest
periodical of which Dom John Stéphan was the founder and editor.
When on his return from the war Fr John was appointed parish priest
of Buckfast, he at once conceived the idea of supplementing his pastoral activities by means of a parish magazine. Like all, or most similar
publications, this organ of publicity consisted of an 'inset'—*Stella
Maris* in this instance—a few pages of local news, and at least one short
article of general interest. Of this magazine the parish priest was the

editor, printer and publisher. The venture proved so successful, that before many months, from a parish magazine it became a quarterly, under the title of *Chimes*, later changed to *Buckfast Abbey Chronicle*. To this more ambitious publication Fr Abbot was a regular contributor—in fact the most regular and dependable of all. A number of essays and articles thus contributed in the course of the years subsequently appeared in book form under the title, respectively, of *The Life of the World to Come*, and *Christianus*.

In the issue of January 1922, the Abbot announced that the solemn inauguration of the church would take place on 2nd July of that year. He then proceeded to relate an incident of his monastic youth: 'One Christmas night I was keeping vigil in the little oratory of the novices —a Bethlehem-like chapel overlooking the foundations of the ancient Abbey church—broad, grey streaks illuminated by the moonlight, as old faces are sometimes lit up by some hope of the future. Peeping through the window at the empty space . . . I asked myself whether it would ever happen that the community, and myself with them, would sing the Midnight Mass on the ancient spot. In the morning I recounted my meditation to the novice-master. He smiled benignly at the dreams of youth.'

He then went on: 'Christmas, this year, will be greater than the dreams of my monastic childhood, for the new church is a bigger thing than I had visualized when gazing at the outlines of the ancient foundations. Mine had been a big Christmas wish, but the wish has been granted, in spite of its formidable proportions.' When these lines were penned, there remained an enormous amount of work to be done if the sequence of solemn functions planned for the first week of August was to be adhered to. One thing is certain—both masons and community never worked so hard as during the first half of that memorable year. At the beginning of July the Abbey annalist wrote: 'Work in the new church is being pushed on as fast as possible. Brothers and workmen start early and leave off late in the evening—after eight o'clock in fact.' The annalist mentions workmen. These were carpenters and other specialists whom we had perforce to employ during those final weeks on jobs that we could not do ourselves. There was a tremendous amount of hammering, concreting of floors and similar disturbances, while the organ-builders were busy with pipes and electric blowers, and a frantic tuner—for whose work quiet was essential—did what he could amid the general din. We were still concreting the floor of the sacristy on the day before the opening. Every day there was a lengthy singing practice, at first by ourselves and, a few days before the opening, jointly with a contingent of choir boys from Westminster Cathedral—fourteen of them.

The inauguration of the Abbey church—incomplete though it was —was regarded by the Catholic body as an event of national significance. Up to this time, out of the many ancient abbeys whose picturesque ruins may be seen in every part of the country, Buckfast alone had been awakened from its long slumber. The event was rightly viewed as a portent and as yet a further proof that the 'Second Spring' was passing into a 'Second Summer'. Our friends accordingly urged us to leave nothing undone in order to stress the significance of the solemn ceremony. It was not difficult to fall in with these wishes seeing that for years our building activities had been brought to the notice of the nation at large, not only by the religious and the local press, but by the big London papers.

The first act in the course of those unforgettable August days was the solemn translation of the statue of Our Lady of Buckfast from the humble temporary church to its new shrine, now all resplendent in the virgin whiteness of its recently restored walls. That triumphant procession, in the golden light of a perfect summer evening, was probably the most picturesque as it was the most thrilling of the many moving functions of that crowded week. Earlier in the afternoon the new church had been blessed and hallowed by the Bishop of Plymouth, who had been a staunch and enthusiastic supporter from the first days of the enterprise. So it was a truly royal progress as the procession wended its way along the leafy lane to the sound of the Litany of Loreto sung with contagious enthusiasm. Eight monks in deacons' dalmatics, strong young men every one of them, carried the statue in relays. On its arrival at the entrance of its new abode the Magnificat was intoned. Rarely can these inspired verses, first sung by our great Queen herself, have seemed more appropriate to the occasion. There were tears of joy and gratitude in many eyes. When at last the noble Figure came to rest in the carved niche above the altar in Mary's own chapel, Arquedelt's *Ave Maria*, sung by the monks and the Westminster choristers, sent a fresh thrill through the vast congregation. 'It was a moment of heaven,' the Abbey annalist wrote, and there were those who claimed that they had seen a smile light up the countenance of our heavenly Queen.

On the following day, from an early hour, crowds of pilgrims and visitors came from far and near, many of whom could not hope to get a seat within the building; many, in fact, never got into the church at all. Cardinal Bourne, who headed a large group of bishops, preached after the gospel of the Mass, taking for his text words from Ezechiel that seemed an inevitable choice for the speaker who would have to give voice to the thoughts of everyone that morning: 'Shall these dry bones live?' That they could live, the Cardinal said, that such a miracle was possible to Him who is life itself, was obvious. Let the listeners but open their eyes and look about them. In the wonderful spectacle of that day the preacher saw an omen for the future, as well as a clear lesson for all. 'When the account of this ceremony goes forth throughout England, surely everyone will ask himself, "What am I doing to make the dry bones live? What response am I making to God, if to me He is saying: I will put my spirit into you, and you shall live?"'

What the Abbot's thoughts were on this day may be gathered from the words he spoke at the luncheon after the Mass. After quoting a French saying to the effect that if you wish to be a builder you must be willing to endure,[1] he said: 'I think we have carried out a great work. It is my only boast, but it will always be my boast, that I started with one pound sterling, and without the promise of any more, but we have gone along and never stopped. You will understand, therefore, that this achievement is not solely due to the men who put their backs into the work, it is also the result of certain things that belong to the moral and spiritual order—I mean trust in God—the beggar's privilege.

'But there is another confidence of which I wish to speak. I have always felt that the tragic death of my predecessor, whose fate I came so near to sharing, was for me a source of spiritual strength, a guarantee that I was meant to accomplish what he was unable to undertake. At the moment of supreme peril I was spared so that I might carry out his heart's desire. I have done it, and it means more to me than if he were alive. . . . I feel I have a right, on this day, to speak of the great secret that is in my heart.' He then briefly referred to the events related in the preceding chapter, and added: 'I would remind you that we have built this great church under conditions which, to human thinking, were almost impossible. We have carried on during the terrible five years of war. . . . British fairness in this crucial period . . . has been one of the glorious things that have enabled us to do the work. I do not think there is any other government in the whole world that would have been so considerate and so kind to us as aliens in your midst as was the British government.'

[1] *Qui veut bâtir doit pâtir.*

It is no exaggeration to say that interest in this event was nation-wide. Buckfast had a very good press! There could be no greater contrast than that between the attitude of a section of the press—the local press that is—less than ten years earlier, and the almost embarrassing tribute of praise and admiration now paid to the community by the national press. One sample, picked almost at random, must suffice.

The Western Morning News, the most important newspaper of the West Country, devoted several columns of its main page to a description of the solemn functions at Buckfast. It also carried a number of excellent photographs and almost verbatim reports of the Cardinal's sermon and the speeches at the luncheon. One of the many items reported by that paper was particularly gratifying. On the Sunday before the opening of the church, the Vicar of St Andrew's, Plymouth's chief Anglican church, referred to Buckfast in his sermon. Preaching from a text taken from 2 Esdras iv. 6 (Neh. iv. 6 in the Revised Version), 'So we built the wall . . . for the people had in mind to work', the preacher said that 'their methods (viz. the Catholics') of presenting the Christian faith may be different from those used in the Anglican Church, but in the building of the great church of Buckfast Abbey by the monks they were given a splendid picture of what even a few could do if they gave themselves heart and soul to a great task.'

The best summing up of public feeling, at least in so far as Catholics were concerned, may be found in a short note of the Cardinal to Fr Abbot, dated 18th August 1922. His Eminence wrote: 'It was indeed a great consolation to be able to give thanks to God with you and your community for the wonderful work that He has enabled you to accomplish. Few days have given me more joy. May He be with you always and grant you to see the full completion of all your hopes and desires. Give me the constant help of your prayers and believe me always your affectionate and devoted servant in J. C.—F. CARD. BOURNE.'

Even so stirring an occurrence as the opening of a new abbey church is only an incident in the even tenor of the life of a religious family. The stir created by the event was outside the enclosure, the calm and orderly routine of community life was only momentarily and superficially ruffled. When one of the visiting bishops observed that after so much excitement and publicity the monks would not easily settle down to the uneventful routine of their days, the Abbot had no difficulty in reassuring His Lordship: 'It will take less than twenty-four hours for everything to return to normal', he said. However, there was a pause of some months in our building activities, in order to give the builders a breathing-space, so to speak, for they had worked against time and under tremendous pressure all through the first half of that year, while it was no less necessary to recover from the considerable expenditure incurred on the occasion of the opening. But what had been achieved was a spur to further effort, and the determination to complete the task was stronger than ever.

The next step was the erection of the west front of the church.

During the pause in the actual building just referred to, much preparatory work was done. The foundations of the west front still lay many feet beneath the surface. They had to be unearthed and covered with a thick layer of concrete. This task occupied many hands for a great many weeks, but at last, on 2nd July 1923, after High Mass, monks and people from the village went in procession to the west end of the church, singing the Litany of our Lady. After the *Veni Creator* had been chanted, the Bishop of Plymouth gave an address in which he once again stated his firm conviction that 'this shrine of our Lady was meant to be a centre of Catholicity, to which people would come to find light and inspiration for their spiritual life.' He then sprinkled the foundations with holy water and thus initiated the second and final phase of the great undertaking.

There is no need to describe this phase in detail, but it is a duty as well as a pleasure to put on record here that Mr and Mrs Schiller, of Wimbledon, made themselves responsible, not only for the whole of the costly west front of the church, but likewise for the fine west gallery, the two chapels, viz. that of St Henry and the Baptistery, as well as for the magnificent stained-glass windows which are so striking a feature of the west end of the church. At a later date, to mark Fr Abbot's silver jubilee as Abbot of Buckfast, Mr Schiller also offered the magnificent baptismal font, 'of the several works of fine craftsmanship at Buckfast perhaps the finest', in the opinion of one well able to judge.[1]

If the Abbey church of Buckfast can be described as an act of faith in stone, it is equally a monument to the spirit of faith, the love of God, and zeal for His glory, of the many benefactors whose self-sacrificing generosity made the work possible. Among these Mr and Mrs Schiller occupy an outstanding place, hence a few biographical details must be set down here—'lest we forget'. Not that there is any danger of this happening since evidence of their truly princely generosity meets the eye both inside and outside the building.

[1] Dom Charles Norris, *Buckfast Abbey Works of Art*, p. 12.

Abbot Vonier made the acquaintance of Mrs Schiller in the course of one of the many retreats he preached at the Convent of the Cenacle, Grayshott. The Abbot's teaching was precisely the spiritual food which this intellectually highly gifted and deeply religious woman longed for. She was also well able to assimilate it. Mrs Schiller's admiration for the Abbot and her love for Buckfast were boundless and her generosity was on a princely scale—in keeping with her motto, 'Only the best is good enough'. The Golden Altar—which has been described as one of the greatest modern masterpieces of the goldsmith's craft—is her personal gift. A little later the Abbot also made the acquaintance of Mr Schiller. This was in 1920. Writing of him in the *Buckfast Abbey Chronicle*, January 1932, the Abbot said: 'Henry Schiller possessed the art of making people happy and of giving opportunely for the amenities of life. He loved the Abbey whole-heartedly.' In point of fact, it is impossible to catalogue his benefactions; for one thing, he made a close secret of his charities. His concern for, and interest in, the Abbey was by no means limited to the building of a major section of the church. To give one or two homely examples: as long as he lived, on all the great feasts of the year, he never failed to send a case of the choicest products of the vineyards he owned in his native Rhineland for the brethren's table. His health, as well as his age, debarred him from every form of sport, but he was fond of indoor games. He loved to entertain and did so *en prince*, but if his guests were dogged by ill-luck at the bridge table he found means to make good those losses in so delicate a fashion that their susceptibilities could not be hurt in the least. 'Uncle Henry', as he was affectionately called—and he knew it and was delighted—was the embodiment of the Christian gentleman as described by Cardinal Newman. 'It is happily within the power of a Benedictine abbey', the Abbot wrote, 'to perpetuate memories more effectively than most institutions. The names of benefactors are inscribed in the hearts of the Brethren, and the story is told by one generation of monks to another.'

On 15th January 1923, Fr Abbot celebrated the Silver Jubilee of his priesthood, though the actual date of his ordination was the 17th December. Eight years later, on 18th October 1931, he completed twenty-five years as Abbot of Buckfast. The event provided a welcome opportunity, not only for the community, but for his innumerable friends and admirers outside, to express their love and admiration for his person and their appreciation of his work. On this occasion, he who was to succeed him so soon in the abbatial office wrote these lines in

Photo, Aero Pictorial Ltd.

BUCKFAST FROM THE AIR

THE ABBEY FROM THE NORTH-WEST

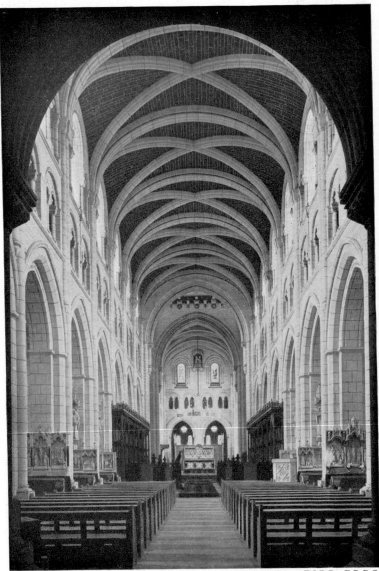

THE INTERIOR OF BUCKFAST ABBEY CHURCH

the *Buckfast Abbey Chronicle*: 'A jubilee is not the end of a career: it is the gathering up of a few of life's achievements into a crown. Coming, as it does, so close to the end of his long years of preparation for a greater event—the consecration of the Abbey church—it provides a most opportune occasion for public acclamation. The solemn consecration will be in itself such a sacred act that personal compliments on that occasion would probably be accepted with embarrassment.'

The celebration of this jubilee was observed as a kind of full-dress rehearsal for that crowning event of the Abbot's career. It was in these very terms that he described it in a letter to the present writer, then at Jerusalem.

What his own feelings were may be gathered from an allocution to the community. It deserves to be rescued from oblivion because it shows how he conceived the abbatial office and the relationship between a Benedictine abbot and his community: 'My twenty-five years of work among you have created in me a burning faith in the greatness of those institutions we call religious communities. A Benedictine abbey is a religious community *par excellence*. There you will find in their fullest extension and power all those elements that make a religious house, the spiritual family, that loom so large in the legislation of the Catholic Church.

'No one could be entrusted with the charge of being the Father of such a family without becoming aware, very soon, of the fact that he is dealing with influences that are not of this world—that he is responsible for interests whose very strangeness makes him tremble. But a quarter of a century of unceasing contact and intimate intercourse with souls . . . is bound to burn into one's deepest consciousness the conviction that one stands in the midst of a great spiritual conflict whose issues are in the hands of God.

'The graces measured out by God to a religious community are well-nigh infinite. . . .

'My work among you has filled me with a burning faith in the greatness of the issues that are at stake in this house, as in every other house of the Order: A religious community has incalculable powers for good: it has an irresistible *charisma* to give edification in the Church of God; its gains are the gains of the whole Church, its losses impoverish the Church herself . . . to have been privileged to do the work of a religious house for so long a period must leave a man profoundly different from what he was at the start; but the most profound feature of that psychological difference, the result of twenty-five years with you, is in my case, I repeat it again, a burning conviction that a religious community is something very great and wonderful in the sight of God, in the sight of God's angels, in the sight of His Catholic Church and, shall we not say it, in the sight of all men.'

CHAPTER IX

THE ABBEY CHURCH IS CONSECRATED

Aedificavit Salomon domum et consummavit eam.—3 Kings vi. 14

WHEN the foundation-stone of the Abbey church was laid by the Bishop of Plymouth on the afternoon of 2nd July 1907, among those who watched the progress of the prelate as he made the circuit of the whole area to be covered by the sacred edifice, there were not a few who said to one another, in no uncertain tones, that they at any rate would not live to see the realization of the immense, not to say impossible task. Yet in 1932, in the spring number of the *Buckfast Abbey Chronicle*, Abbot Anscar had the intense satisfaction of announcing that the church would be consecrated on 25th August of that year: 1932 was to be the *annus mirabilis* for Buckfast. 'There is no man so prosaic,' the Abbot wrote, 'as not to ask himself a question or two in his first wakeful hour on the first day of the New Year. What will it bring forth? The pious, even more than the ordinary run of people, ply the New Year with questions. Happily for them the opening contains more certainties than for most. The year is no enigma, no sphinx, for the splendour of the Faith will fill each of its days more surely than the sunshine its hours of light. Sunshine only goes by averages, even in Devon, whilst faith is ever a maximum. For a long time we have looked forward to 1932 as the year in which Buckfast Abbey church would be consecrated. There was in the choice of 1932 something of the lightheartedness which makes a man accept unflinchingly obligations which will not be pressed for a very long term.'

At last the dreams, hopes and prayers, not to speak of the sweat and toil of a quarter of a century, were to have their glorious reward. Though on that New Year's Day much remained to be done, the sacred edifice would somehow be ready for the sublime ritual by which a building reared by man's hands becomes for ever the house and property of the God who inhabits eternity.

In this country we are familiar with ceremonial 'openings' of churches and chapels. But there is a whole world's difference between an opening and a dedication, or consecration. However vast the concourse of clergy and people on the occasion of an opening, the edifice lacks something that consecration alone can confer upon it. By that imposing ritual God is put in sole possession of the edifice; its title-deeds, so to speak, are handed over to Him, so that at no time may it be put to profane uses. One all-important prerequisite for such a transaction between man and God is that the building be free of debt. That condition was happily fulfilled in this instance, for no money had ever been borrowed. Ours had been a hand-to-mouth undertaking in the sense that we never undertook more than we were able to pay for.

On 30th December of the previous year, in a letter to Dourgne, the Abbot had said: 'The year that is about to begin must be a year of grace, in view of the consecration of our Abbey church. I view it chiefly as a triumph of faith. These twenty-five years of toil have cut a deep furrow in the mentality of the community. Your community is already fixed in a state of perfection, whereas we are still striving to attain perfection [1]; but both states have their own graces. There is spiritual beauty in a religious body contending with difficulties as there is beauty in a life where all is peace and prosperity.' By prosperity, in the present context, he obviously meant not so much temporal prosperity as a life free from pressing anxiety.

The impending consecration of the church called forth enormous interest, not only in Devonshire, but all over the country. Locally the most extravagant rumours were current both as to the number and the importance of the people who would attend the solemn function. Rumour even had it that the Pope would perform the ceremony in person.[2]

In spite of its obvious absurdity, so widespread was the rumour that as early as March 1931 the Abbot General wrote to the Abbot that in a recent audience with Pius XI, he had informed His Holiness of the consecration of the church in 1932, and that he had even mentioned the above rumours. 'We shall go by aeroplane,' the Pontiff observed with a chuckle. However, he at once declared that since he could not officiate in person, he would commission Cardinal Bourne to do so in his name. This was the first intimation we had of Pius XI's intention

---

[1] The allusion is to the theologians' distinction between what they call *status perfectionis acquirendae*, which is said to be the state of religious, and *status perfectionis acquisitae*, which is that of bishops, by reason of their office and position in the Church.

[2] The manageress of a hotel in a town that shall be nameless wrote to say that she would do her very best for the Pope and any other important personages for whom we would wish to find particularly good accommodation.

to honour Buckfast and the Archbishop of Westminster by appointing him his Legate *a latere* for the great occasion. On 21st March, feast of St Benedict, a telegram signed by Cardinal Pacelli—now Pius XII gloriously reigning—brought official notification of the Legate's nomination, as well as the further information that in view of Cardinal Bourne's indifferent health, His Holiness permitted him to pass on to some other prelate the arduous task of the actual consecration and the celebration of the Mass that would follow. This would enable the Legate to husband his strength for the sermon he was to preach, which, so we were told, would have 'un carattere singolarmente significativo'.

That the Cardinal felt highly honoured by the appointment may be gathered from a letter to the Abbot: 'I know well', he wrote, 'that it is to you that I owe the great honour which is to be conferred upon me. . . . I am very grateful for this distinction and also that it should be arranged in such a way as not to entail upon me undue fatigue. It is a great satisfaction to me that other bishops should be associated with me on this very great occasion.'

While the honour done to the Archbishop of Westminster was a striking proof of the high esteem in which he was held in Rome, it was also meant to redound upon Buckfast. But, not content with this magnificent gesture, Pius XI decided to honour the Abbot of Buckfast by a personal mark of esteem. This His Holiness did when, by a Brief of 8th August, signed by Cardinal Pacelli, then Secretary of State, he granted to him the personal privilege of the use of the *Cappa Magna*. Though cast in the customary mould of the curial style, the Brief strikes a personal note when it refers to the Abbot's building activities and to the books by which he had so admirably promoted the Catholic Faith.

This recognition of his work by the highest authority on earth gave Dom Anscar immense satisfaction. Thereafter he never missed an opportunity of appearing in that stately but, to the onlooker, somewhat cumbersome ornament. The honour had been asked for by the Abbot General, hence the Abbot obviously viewed the gracious act as a silent but significant gesture of approval of his administration, which, in point of fact, had not escaped criticism and, at times, downright misrepresentation.

At last the longed-for day of the dedication dawned. It was to be a very long day and an exciting one, but twenty-five years of arduous toil had kept everyone in training. The day began at three in the

morning when Matins, Lauds and Prime were recited, after which the
priests said their Masses at improvised altars in the former church, by
now the library. This was not one of the least joys of that happy day,
for that homely building held sweet and holy memories for most of the
priests since it was within its walls that nearly all of them had pronounced their monastic vows and received the crowning grace of the
priesthood.

The first scene of the vast pageant that was to unfold itself that day
before an immense concourse of people had been acted on the previous
evening, when the Papal Legate was solemnly received at the west
doors of the new church. The whole village was beflagged in his
honour. From medieval Dart Bridge up to the Abbey festoons and
banners made a triumphal road for the representative of the Head
of the Church, and over the ancient south gate of the Abbey a Latin
inscription greeted the Legate: *Ave, Misse Sancti Petri*—'Hail, envoy
of St Peter!' it said. And, indeed, what is the Pope but *Perpetuus
Petrus*, the immortal Rock on which Christ our Lord built His Church?
When the Legate had been escorted up the nave, into the chancel, the
Papal Brief of appointment was read, after which the Abbot addressed
the Legate. Abbot Anscar rarely betrayed his feelings, but at this
moment his accustomed self-control failed him and it was in a voice
strangled by emotion that he now spoke, so much so indeed that only
those fairly close to him were able to follow his words. His address
must be given in full since it reveals what was in his mind in that hour
—an hour we may well call the greatest of his whole life since it
marked the consummation of the task for which God had so obviously
prepared and so providentially preserved him. He spoke as follows:

'When I behold the spectacle which now meets my eyes, I am truly
filled with confusion. You have come here, my Lord Cardinal, as the
representative of the greatest power on earth. You are here among us
with all the majesty of the throne of Peter. The supreme spiritual
authority honours us in the person of Your Eminence. There are
assembled here many of your brethren in the episcopate, forming a
cortège worthy of a Legate *a latere*, of one who comes, as it were, from
the very presence of the Supreme Pontiff. What have I done to deserve
such an honour? What has my community done to be thus singled
out by the Vicar of Christ for so exceptional a privilege? I say it in all
sincerity, my Lord Cardinal, I feel oppressed by the greatness of the
favour. Yet there is in my heart something that reassures me in the
midst of this undeserved preference, and I make so bold as to say that

I feel in reality that what is now happening is the reward for things done. You will not be surprised to hear me make such a profession of confidence. All that you see here has been an act of faith. This church about to be consecrated is truly the fruit of faith. Our faith has been simple, unquestioning, childlike. We have had no other talent or genius except the talent or genius of faith. Now it is not pride but loyalty to Christ to boast of our faith; faith is the one virtue whose possession we may proclaim from the housetop. We have had faith, and we are proud of having had it.

'Is it not Peter's particular glory to love faith? to praise faith wherever it is to be found? Peter is the man of faith, not only in the sense of his being the custodian of dogmatic orthodoxy, but also in the sense of his trust in Christ, unreserved, unquestioning.

'We all love to sum up the mighty mission of our Holy Father, Pope Pius XI, in the prophetic words *Fides intrepida*; is there a man in the world of greater faith than the Pontiff who sends you to us? This gift of faith, then, which has been our only power, makes us share in the spirit of Peter himself. Speaking boldly, may I not say that faith establishes a bond of dignity between the Supreme Pontiff and the least of his sons? In sending Your Eminence to us His Holiness has honoured our faith; he has recognized in it something that makes us worthy of him. We consider, therefore, Your Eminence's presence here, not in the light of an overpowering majesty, but in the light of a glorious spiritual fellowship. You come here as the reward of our faith, and may I hope that your abiding amongst us will be to Your Eminence personally an increase of "the joy in believing".'

The ceremonies of the consecration began at half past six on the following morning, while a biting east wind chilled everyone to the bone, but it was a happy omen of fine weather and before long the sun was shining out of a cloudless sky. The age-old rites of the dedication filled all the hours of the morning and it was only by midday that they came to an end. After an interval the Mass of the dedication began. By this time well over a thousand people had somehow found at least standing room within the edifice all fragrant with the perfume of its recent consecration. Several thousand more had of necessity to remain outside—but by means of loudspeakers they too were able to follow the service and to hear the memorable sermon of the Legate after the gospel of the Mass. The B.B.C. had requested permission to broadcast this address, which had indeed 'un carattere singolarmente significativo' and was surely one of the most inspiring of Cardinal

Bourne's many public utterances. Speaking in the quiet tones that were so admirably in keeping with the character and personality of 'The Quiet Cardinal', as his biographer styles him, His Eminence reminded his vast seen and unseen audience of the circumstances which led to the return of the monks to this hallowed spot. With these details the reader is already acquainted, but a few passages of the address have their place here, were it only that they will enable the reader to recapture something of the thrills of that great occasion:

'We stand on holy ground,' the Cardinal said, 'beneath which lie buried the servants of God who in this place, for long centuries, raised up before the throne of God a hymn of praise and supplication; who, while living by the labour of their hands, made the earth more fruitful, and gave to their fellow men an ever-present incitement to useful, industrious and God-fearing living. These old-time monks, whether Saxon or Norman, Benedictine or Cistercian, are with us—who can doubt it?—to join their voices with ours in the chant of liturgy and psalmody, in oneness of faith and worship. We are at home with them, they are at home with us, in all those things which really matter in the service of Almighty God. . . .

'In the nature of human things there was no reason why the work which had begun before the Norman Conquest should not have continued until now. They (the monks of old) were true to their monastic life, they had a long and honourable history. But they were destined not to escape the destruction which a lustful, covetous king was determined to inflict on all the religious houses of our country. . . . The overthrow of Buckfast was but one item in the fundamental change which Henry VIII wrought in the ecclesiastical constitution of England, making it clearly schismatical so far as it was in his power to do so, and thus preparing the way for the setting up of the definitely heretical Elizabethan Establishment outside the unity of the Western Church. Thus the old Abbey of Buckfast became a ruin, a ruin so complete that all trace of it seemed to be lost for ever. Its sacred stones were gradually pilfered for domestic purposes, and no one dreamed of a time when the Abbey should live again.'

After recounting the story of Père Muard, the expulsion from La Pierre-qui-Vire and the return of the monks on 28th October 1882, the Cardinal went on:

'God acts in His own way. There was one, only a boy of seven, when Buckfast first resumed its old monastic state, who since then had been prepared by the Divine will to re-establish its ancient glories.

I cannot say, in his presence, all that is his due—but his rejoicing and his thanksgiving must be of a rare quality as he gazes on his Abbey today. The Providence which had prepared him has traced his path throughout the years since 1906. . . .'

The Cardinal then went on to refer to the celebration of the centenaries of several ancient abbeys, 'by those,' he said, 'who can claim neither connexion nor continuity of thought or doctrine with the men who set them up, but who are obliged to recognize, however reluctantly, as spiritual progenitors the men who cast them down. . . . With all suchlike commemorations the consecration of St Mary's Church at Buckfast stands in conspicuous and magnificent contrast. It reaches across the long years of obscurity, of patient endurance, of heroic perseverance, of faithfulness unto death; it links up again the old religion of the English people, which made England what she is; with its present revival in our midst . . . it shows forth the power of the Catholic Church to triumph over the ruins of the past, to piece together the broken fragments, to overcome the powers of evil, to bring forth renewal from the most devastating efforts of those who hate God, and His Christ, and His Church.'

In a moving conclusion the Legate addressed the Abbot directly: 'You enter today, my dear Father Abbot, into possession of your church consecrated for ever to the service of Him to whom you and your community have dedicated by solemn vow the homage of your whole life. A great charge is entrusted to you to make of your Abbey, as the Holy Father reminds you,[1] a home of religion, of piety, and of learning, shining forth amidst all the uncertainties and perplexities that affect men's minds today; to set up and maintain in our midst a haven of rest, wherein by constant, unceasing prayer and holiness of life, the minds and hearts of our fellow countrymen may be drawn to understand better, to examine more closely, to approach without prejudice, to seek in earnest prayer, and ultimately, by God's grace, to accept and practise that Catholic Faith whence came forth the Buckfast Abbey upon the ruins of which that same Faith, and the courage which that Faith inspires, have built this glorious Abbey of today.'

A description of the new church and its beautiful furnishings would be out of place in these pages and for this I would refer the reader to a delightful little book by an expert.[2] An appreciation, however, of the edifice by so competent a writer as the late Ernest Oldmeadow, the

[1] In the Brief granting him the privilege of the *Cappa Magna*.
[2] *Buckfast Abbey: A Pictorial Survey*, by Dom Charles Norris, Buckfast Abbey.

then editor of *The Tablet*, may be quoted because it does much more than describe the building—it puts into words the impression it makes, or is calculated to make, on a sensitive visitor. Writing in *The Tablet* of 3rd September 1932, pp. 315 ff., Mr Oldmeadow begins by affirming that 'not only does Buckfast Abbey church "take" poorly as an architectural photograph, but it suffers heavy loss from being seen, as most people see it, with visitors moving about. On Thursday night [viz. 25th August], at the always quiet and refreshing hour of Compline, I stole into the church after the pilgrims and trippers had gone home, and early the next morning, before any trippers were about, I spent some hours there while Masses were being said at all the fifteen altars . . . only then did I grasp the fullness of Frederick Walters' success. His church is for monks to do their work in, not for travellers to come and look at.

'I have just said "for monks to do their work in". The *Opus Dei* of a Benedictine family is work as truly as the work of a farm or a factory, and the impression made by the common-sense, practical, square-ended choir, with its handsome yet sturdy triforium, is an impression that might almost be called business-like. If I may use homely language, here is a place for Almighty God's operatives "to get on with it"—a workshop for the *Opus Dei*.

'The useful and the beautiful do not exclude one another—on the contrary, a building designed for use is nearly always better than a primarily ornamental pile. I have called the church at Buckfast a workshop; and, none the less, its interior is beautiful, as to both its proportion and its parts.'

To this vivid description of the 'character', or, what may be called the 'atmosphere' of the Abbey church many more might be added did space permit. Mr Edward Hutton, in an article in *The Nineteenth Century and After*, which, by courtesy of the Editor was printed in full in the *Buckfast Abbey Chronicle*, has some very fine things to say: 'The beautiful Abbey of Our Lady of Buckfast, built by the hands of its own monks within the last twenty-six years, seems like an apparition and a portent. As though from the tragic ruins of so many such places, which still ennoble the English landscape with their beauty even in death, one at least had re-arisen—yes, from the very foundations of its predecessor; as though the very stones had towered up and bloomed again in pillar and capital and arch, and there it stood amid the trees, mirrored once more in the stream, served as of old by the monks in this Devonshire valley. And one asks oneself, as one looks at it in the ineffable peace of an English summer evening amid the woods and green pastures, beside the loveliness of the Dart, what does it mean? Can it be that that which made it in the beginning, the Faith which founded it, is returning—after four hundred years? . . . meeting the monks in this Devonshire valley, how can one escape recalling what this England we love so much, England especially, owes to the sons of St Benedict? Nothing less than Christianity itself.'

The concluding lines of this delightful article are even more striking: 'Standing there in the sight of Buckfast—*sicut cervus ad fontes* (Buckfast's motto) on those moonlight nights when Compline is over . . . almost anything seems possible. Buckfast itself is little short of a miracle, a resurrection from the dead, if ever there was one.' And as if the wings of the Spirit that prompted the prophets of old were hovering about him in the bright moonlight by the banks of the Dart, the writer hints at a future even more splendid than England's monastic past: 'Even now,' he writes, 'there are more choir monks at Downside today than there were at Glastonbury before the Suppression; there are more too at Ampleforth now than there were at Rievaulx and Fountains together. Moreover, with the development of elementary education and the means of travel, many people seem to have taken up a different attitude in regard to these things from that of their forefathers, or even their parents. But the future is hidden from man. At least here, as by a miracle, stands once more in all its beauty beside the stream the thousand-year-old Abbey of Our Lady of Buckfast. *Esto perpetua!*'

Perhaps even more striking is the tribute paid to the Abbot and his community by the *Daily Mail*, which, in addition to some excellent pictures, had a leading article so full of understanding of what one may call the inner spirit of the enterprise that it warmed the heart almost more effectively than anything said and written on that memorable occasion. One or two paragraphs from that very fine article may suitably bring this chapter to a close: 'The work of untiring hands, to which religious enthusiasm gave a purpose and enduring strength, must stand through the centuries to come as a precious example of the simple faith moving mountains. It is an achievement on which the Roman Catholic Church can deservedly be congratulated.

'Romance and high piety are inseparably mingled in this epic of self-help. The monks who builded had the spirit of medieval artisans. They laboured from sunrise to sunset, and had joy of their work, **because they believed it hallowed.'** [1]

---

[1] The heavy type is as in the original article.

At the conclusion of the moving tribute which the late Bishop Keily of Plymouth, then Canon Keily, paid to his great friend Dom Boniface Natter, on the occasion of the solemn Requiem for one whose grave is the mighty deep, he spoke these words: 'No one knows the future, but somehow or other from such an end of self-sacrifice we can expect anything from the Providence of God . . . perchance the old walls will rise again . . . perhaps there will be found here one day a splendid house of God. . . .' Prophetic words splendidly fulfilled! What is more, unlike what befell in the days of Zorobabel, the new shrine seems to surpass in beauty the one destroyed in the sixteenth century: *O matre pulchra filia pulchrior!* The abbeys that once adorned our countryside are but picturesque ruins, mourning their glorious past on the hillsides or in the lovely valleys, where even in decay they retain power to attract the curious tourist and the thoughtful student of bygone days. To Mary's shrine at Buckfast, and to it alone up till then, had the Author of life spoken a quickening *talitha cumi!* and at His bidding life had returned, and more abundant life, where the sleep of death had seemingly settled for ever. We who witnessed the miracle can but repeat, with those who once prayed, sang, joyed, suffered and toiled on this spot but have long ago joined the heavenly choirs, the joyful cry of Holy Church: *Regem cui omnia vivunt, venite adoremus!* [1]

[1] Two fine churches were also built during Abbot Vonier's abbacy, the one at Buckfastleigh and the other at Ashburton, chiefly through the exertions of the zealous parish priest of that period, Dom John Stéphan. On the other hand, the flourishing mission of Totnes was handed over to the bishop of the diocese. A site for a church has also been acquired at South Brent and Mass has been said there for many years. Buckfast Abbey held land there in pre-Reformation times.

CHAPTER X

THE WRITER

In the early autumn of 1937 Abbot Vonier assisted for the last time at a chapter of the French Province of the Cassinese Congregation, for within a few weeks of that gathering Buckfast was to be detached from the French Province to become a unit of the English Province together with Prinknash and St Augustine's Abbey, Ramsgate. The chapter was held at Saint-Benoît-sur-Loire, near Orleans, in the shadow of the venerable romanesque basilica which houses the relics of St Benedict—or at least a considerable portion of them. When the Abbot's administration came up for review by the assembly—during which the Abbot left the room—the chairman began by expressing his amazement at the fact that a man whose time and energy were so fully engaged by so many heavy commitments of a purely material order, could yet find time to produce a new book almost every year, and he frankly confessed that though he was not engaged in building a church, a feat of this kind would nevertheless be beyond his powers.

Many a reader who has followed this story up to this point will share that good prelate's astonishment, for amid the ceaseless demands made upon his time Abbot Vonier wrote no less than fifteen books, of which at least one may be described as epoch-making. Abbot Vonier possessed an imposing exterior; his intellectual stature was on a par with the physical. He passionately loved the things of the mind, if such an expression is in order when speaking of one who seemed at all times wrapped in Olympian calm. One explanation of his remarkable literary output—it is only a partial one—is that though his mental gifts were of a rare quality, and his interest in the things of the spirit boundless, he kept his intellectual curiosity under strict control, just as he did the whole of his conduct. He was fully aware of his outstanding talent and of his ability to take any one branch of knowledge in his stride. Thus, at one period, shortly after his return from his year's studies in Rome, he took up the study of mathematics, and at this time he told me that if he cared, or had the time, he could easily master what for most people is a dry and abstruse subject—higher mathematics. However, a monk, or a priest, may not pursue erudition for its own sake; his is a dedicated life, so that he is not free to dispose of his time as he pleases but must apply himself to such pursuits as serve the ultimate purpose of his vocation. Dom Anscar was of the number of those who, in the words of St Bernard, 'seek knowledge in order that they may benefit others, and such a pursuit of wisdom is born of charity, while there are others who seek it for their own personal advantage and they are actuated by prudence'.[1]

The study of theology was Dom Anscar's great love and to it he remained faithful to the end of his days. Theology is the priest's professional knowledge, and like all other intellectual pursuits it demands a thorough preparation, a sound knowledge of the classical languages, especially Latin, being one of the essential requisites. As a matter of fact, if the future priest devotes several years to the study of Latin and Greek, he does not do so for a purely utilitarian end. The priest ought to be versed, not only in theology, but likewise in those humane arts which are the basis of real culture. Notwithstanding the claims of the advocates of an almost exclusively scientific or technical education, ability to read the Greek and Latin classics remains an indispensable ingredient of true mental culture. Dom Anscar's fluent Latin never failed to call forth admiration at gatherings at which Latin was the only language understood by all its members. Among the very few books that occupied a permanent place on his writing-table there was a Horace and Cicero's De Legibus. Unless memory plays me false, the last conversation I had with him, or at any rate one of the very last, was a discussion of one of Tibullus' lyrics.

Dom Anscar's Roman experience, short though it was, undoubtedly proved a turning-point in his career. Though he read philosophy and took a doctor's degree in that noble science, theology was the abiding interest of his life. But to Sant' Anselmo he owed a great deal more than an academic degree, hence his interest in that great Benedictine centre of learning never waned. The very first of his many letters to the Abbess of Dourgne, written a few days after his return to Buckfast after his rescue from the waters of the Mediterranean, dealt with Sant' Anselmo.

In his capacity of Visitor of the French Province, Abbot Boniface Natter had been at pains to persuade Superiors to send some of their

---

[1] *Sunt qui scire volunt ut aedificent, et charitas est; et item qui scire volunt ut aedificentur, et prudentia est*—(In Cant. sermo 36).

young subjects to Rome. In the case of the Abbot of En Calcat his pleading fell on deaf ears. Abbot Romanus Banquet flatly refused to allow any one of his young monks to go to an establishment which, in his eyes, would undermine the particular spirit and outlook which he sought to instil into his monastic family. The Abbot of En Calcat was undoubtedly a man of God, but he did not possess the charisma of broad-mindedness. One example will suffice to prove that this is not a calumny of his memory. When his community was forced to seek refuge in Spain, in consequence of anti-religious laws, he would not allow anyone to learn the language of the country and he saw to it that there was neither Spanish grammar nor dictionary in the house. To such a man the ethos of an international college like Sant' Anselmo could not fail to be suspect. So to the abbess of the sister-abbey Dom Anscar wrote: 'I have told you of the desire that was uppermost in the heart of Rt Rev. Dom Boniface on what was to be the last day of his life and about which he intended to write to you, when he was called to his reward.' This desire was that the Abbess, who wielded enormous influence over Abbot Banquet, should press the latter to be more forthcoming on the question of sending students to Rome. 'I believe,' Dom Anscar went on, 'that the thing is of great importance. If the best of our young men are deprived of the finish which the higher education provided by Rome can impart, we [viz. the French Province] shall be condemned to a position of mediocrity in our Congregation.' He then alludes to the fact that Abbot Natter attached great virtue to the Abbess's wisdom and experience, so much so indeed that he was wont to call her his permanent co-Visitor.[1] 'For this reason', Dom Anscar wrote, 'Abbot Natter had a right to demand that you use your influence in order to give effect to his last wishes.'

In view of the recruiting of its members, a Benedictine monastery is a kind of miniature university in which most branches of learning are taught—more especially philosophy and theology. Dom Anscar was accordingly engaged in teaching from the day of his ordination. For such a task he was admirably equipped, for he was not only learned himself but he had the gift of imparting his knowledge to others—an ability not invariably possessed by the erudite. Dom Anscar was a born teacher and lecturer; for one thing he was endowed with boundless patience which would not suffer him to let the less gifted students limp as best they might behind the clever ones.

[1] When holding a canonical visitation, the Visitor must have a *Socius*—else the visitation would be irregular and uncanonical.

Experience seems to prove that teaching rouses and stimulates the urge to write. Abbot Anscar regarded his literary activity as part of the mission with which Providence had charged him. The supreme aim of his life was undoubtedly the spread of God's Kingdom in the land of his adoption. The rebuilding of the ancient Abbey church and the adjoining monastery was but one half of his programme, important though it was. For him the publication of a new book was as gratifying an experience as the completion of a major section of the church. How often one has heard him say: 'We must write spiritual books instinct with doctrine—we must give the people solid theology, for they hunger for such spiritual food'. So it was neither for fame nor money that he subjected himself to the arduous discipline of the pen. How exacting that discipline is can only be fully appreciated by those who have themselves spent long hours at the writing-table. Horace compares the would-be writer to a runner in the stadium who needs must undergo severe training if he would compete with a hope of success.[1]

Talent is needed, but so is arduous and sustained application. I have already said that Dom Anscar was exceptionally gifted. His was a lucid, sensitive and penetrating intelligence, while the gravity of his character prevented him from frittering away his time and energy on reading and study that would not serve his ultimate purpose. He was well aware of the power of the spoken word, but he also realized that from its very nature it is evanescent whereas the written word retains its virtue even as the dry and shrivelled petals of the rose continue to yield their fragrance after the glory of their brilliant hues has departed. In addition to a personal urge, pressure was also brought to bear on him by people who longed for a deeper knowledge of the things of God. As a matter of fact he was most willing to gratify such longings: 'Keenness for knowledge,' he writes, 'is the surest sign of a healthy mental constitution, while listlessness and indifference to the things of the intellect argues more than mental paralysis: it is a positive depravity of the heart; the heart has become heavy through indulgence of the senses and it loathes the effort which is demanded by all true knowledge' (Collected Works, Vol. III, p. 321). In the chapter of the book from which this quotation is taken he does not hesitate to say that 'knowledge, more knowledge, knowledge without any limit—such is the view Catholic theology takes of man's destiny. Man is born to know as the beast of burden is born to labour. . . . In God's

---

[1] Qui studet optatam cursu contingere metam
Multa tulit fecitque puer, sudavit et alsit.

providence knowledge comes to man gradually, wave after wave, but a day will come when man will be fit for all knowledge, and that day will be the first in the life of the world to come' (*ibid.*, p. 323). It cannot be otherwise, since, as Dante has it, eternal death is the loss of that which constitutes the bliss of the intellect—for the reprobate are:

> *genti dolorose*
> *ch'hanno perduto il ben dell' intelletto,*

wretched people who have lost the good of the intellect.

It was in the year 1911 that Abbot Vonier began work on the first of his many books, the subject being the human soul. The greater part of the book must have been written during the winter months of that year, when the season guarded him somewhat against the endless interruptions of which one in his position and with so many commitments on his hands was bound to be the victim.[1] It was interesting to watch him at work. The thousands who have benefited by his books no doubt picture him as seated at a table littered with books, or with books within easy reach. The reality was very different. Apart from the Bible, the *Summa* of St Thomas, the two Latin volumes already mentioned, and an English dictionary, I do not think he had as many as a dozen books in his room. *The Human Soul* was written, not at his desk, but in an easy chair, on long, single sheets. The book seemed to write itself; sheet after sheet was filled with astonishing speed and, apparently, without effort, and almost before the ink was dry a noble lady tapped them out on her typewriter. Most of his books were produced by a similar process, but those of the last years of his life were dictated to a devoted assistant who at times successfully argued with him on points of style and grammar. It is probable that this procedure is responsible for some of his stylistic shortcomings. These blemishes cannot be denied, but the reader soon forgets them, gripped as he is by the absorbing interest of the subject-matter.

There are those who regard *The Human Soul* as the Abbot's best work. The title should not lead anyone to think that the book is only another of those stuffy volumes on psychology which clutter the bookstalls these days. Abbot Vonier had taken a doctor's degree in philosophy and, had he been so minded, could easily have added yet another 'popular' manual to the many already in existence. But for him the writing of books was part of his priestly activity. His book is indeed a

[1] In a letter to the Abbess of Dourgne, dated 17th December 1913, he speaks of his literary activity and the difficulties under which it was carried on: 'My time is so chopped up'! and he adds, 'my head is very often a burden to me'. This is an obvious reference to the headaches which in these years almost paralysed him at times.

profound analysis of the origin, nature and destiny of the human soul —but he does not, as it were, insulate his subject in order to study it apart from the human personality. Man is not a soul, the soul is not man. The human person is compounded of soul and body, spirit and matter, so that it is in very deed a compendium or abridgment of all God's works. Hence, in spite of the title of the book, the Abbot studies the human soul, not in the abstract, but as it exists and functions as the dominant element of the human personality. The book is a study of man both in the light of reason and in the brighter splendour of divine revelation. In that medium man is seen to be, in St Augustine's magnificent phrase, 'an earthy being, but one fit for heaven'—*terrenum animal, sed coelo dignum* (*De Civ. Dei*, PL, XXII, 1). The book supplies the answer to practically every question about the soul and its destiny that may arise in the mind of a thoughtful Christian. In this work the Abbot displays a youthful freshness and vigour, and though his theme bristles with abstruse metaphysical problems, such is his grasp of his subject that he is able to explain the most subtle topics in language that an educated person should not find it difficult to understand.

The Human Soul may be described as a synthesis of all we know about man's origin and destiny. The author speaks in accents of persuasive eloquence about the high destiny that awaits him after the brief episode of this earthly existence. Man, the creature of an eternal God, is himself, so to speak, instinct with eternity. His soul only unfolds all its powers in the world for which it is really destined—God's own world. A quotation or two, chosen almost at random, will give the reader a good idea of the rich food for mind and heart that this valuable book provides. When describing what he calls the soul's 'awakening', that is, the time when a human being comes to what is called the age of reason, he writes: 'To understand more clearly the kind of awakening there is in the human soul, we must bear in mind the far-reaching principle that "the soul is to the body a principle of higher life". To be such a principle is, so to speak, the whole *raison d'être* of the soul. The soul is essentially a spiritual leaven to the body, permeating the mass of the human organism. The moment the soul begins that leavening it is fully active, it fulfils its mission completely. Even in the embryonic human individual the soul is indefatigably at work as the principle of a growth that soon will result in the mature human brain, with its super-sensitive powers and operations. The soul has not to awake: it is the bodily organism that has to awake; the soul's mission is to bring about that higher awakening of the brain which makes man superior to the animal . . . man is superior to the animal through his higher sensitive life, through his higher sensitive consciousness, as well as through his intellectual life . . . but as for itself, the soul always remains a hidden principle as long as it is united with the body' (*Coll. Works*, III, 24 f.).

This passage is a fair sample of matter, manner and style. We may note the absence of abstruse terminology, the limpidity of the exposition, but likewise the looseness and repetitiveness of the phrasing. The fact is that the Abbot wrote as he spoke—this is how he lectured. For a proper appraisal of his writings we should regard them as reports of lectures, and not even as very carefully revised and amended reports. He spoke slowly, with his mind in travail for the right word, the appropriate image or comparison that would best embody the thought that stood in sharply defined outlines before his mind. So long as he succeeded in 'getting it across', little did he care about style. That he was hampered by the necessity of finding equivalents for Latin or Greek terms is obvious. Ability to expound deep theology without the help of the technical vocabulary devised by 'our Masters', as the Abbot used to call the great scholastic theologians of the past, was one of his outstanding gifts, though technical terms actually clutter many a page. Their use was all but inescapable, and so familiar were they to him that he may have imagined the reader to be on equally easy terms with the language of the schools. That he was profoundly conscious of the need of a clearly defined terminology if ambiguity in these lofty questions is to be avoided may be gathered from a letter to a Benedictine nun who had consulted him on the meaning of certain terms which he could not help using. The letter is a good sample of his epistolary style. Though he had known his consultant for years, the letter is quite impersonal. 'Substance,' he writes, 'in Catholic theology means essence, the very nature and reality of a thing. An angel is a spiritual substance; man is a substance composed of body and soul. God is an infinite spiritual substance. In English the term is sadly degraded and means things material, tangible, like a substantial cheque. So when it is said in the Creed that the Son is of the same substance with the Father, the meaning is that the Son and the Father have the same nature, the same essence, the same life.

'But all our terms are being made vile—essence is petrol, substance is fatness, personality is oddity, redemption and conversion are banking operations. It shows how indispensable the use of Latin is to the preservation of ideas in the world.'

In view of these reflections another quotation will be of interest since it deals with a particularly subtle theme—the Beatific Vision. The difficulty of explaining this glorious climax of the story of the human soul to people who find it hard to breathe in this rarefied theological atmosphere is obvious. Abbot Vonier made the attempt in one of the most inspiring chapters of his book. 'The main idea conveyed by the term "Beatific Vision" is this: it is God, as He is in Himself, who is seen by the mind; it is not a mere image of Him, a mere idea of Him, however clear; it is Himself. It is a direct, uninterrupted gazing on God's beauty. . . . In the Beatific Vision, according to the profound doctrine of St Thomas, God Himself becomes the idea which is in the mind of the elect. All our cognitions are ideas that come to our mind through a hundred channels. We see clearly that the idea of a thing is not the thing itself, for the thing is outside me, whilst the idea is in my mind . . . in the Beatific Vision there is no such idea of God, as distinct from God, to stand for God in my mind. If I am to know Him as He is, He Himself must be the idea that makes my mind a knowing mind.'

However 'to see God for ever' is a phrase that does not give the whole content of the theological doctrine. 'We must not think of that glorious life as of an endless succession and repetition of the same act, so that to see God for ever would be merely to see Him day by day, for ever and ever. The Vision of God is eternal life . . . "eternal" here, has a technical and exclusive meaning. We must define eternity thus: the actual, total and unchanging possession of life. Unchangeableness, and totality of all happiness in that unchangeableness, is God's eternity. It is not so much an endless life as an unchangeable life. . . .' (*Coll. Works*, III, 141 f.).

It cannot be said that this is easy reading; but it is not unintelligible. For this unimaginable Vision of God, the human soul must be further strengthened, or spiritualized. This is done by what is called 'the light of glory'—*lumen gloriae*—which floods the soul with its brightness and enables it to gaze without flinching into the splendour of the eternal Sun of Justice. 'Frequent reflection on this possible eternity for our created, ever-changing minds,' the Abbot writes, 'may become for us the source of great spiritual strength. The emptiness which constant change of emotion leaves behind will make the thoughtful happy in the belief in a state so perfect that its eternal stability is its eternal newness' (*Coll. Works*, III, 147).

One reviewer of the book, after stating that 'there is a delightful freshness in not a few chapters, an unconventionality of expression and at times a happy choice of phrase that cannot fail to please', goes on to observe that the author 'has not escaped the great danger which besets all popular expositions of technical points: simplicity is not synonymous with clearness and precision . . . his readers cannot fail to be troubled by the indiscriminate intermingling of pure philosophy and theology.'

It is not my business to defend Abbot Vonier, but it is precisely this presentation of the subject that constitutes the interest—I might say the originality—of his book. Since man's whole destiny is ordained to a supernatural end—and it is from that point of view that the Abbot studies him—he was bound to focus the twin lights of philosophy and theology upon him. The reviewer ends by saying that 'the theologian will find the book stimulating, but whether the educated layman will find it as helpful as the learned author means it to be is open to doubt'. These doubts were unjustified. It may be said that while the book, as well as those that came after it, did not invariably escape criticism, those for whom the books were written hailed them with enthusiasm.

The Human Soul was the first of a trilogy of major works. The next was *The Personality of Christ*, published shortly after the outbreak of the First World War. Abbot Vonier cherished what I might call a Pauline love and devotion for the Person of Christ. Those who knew him best felt that it was only a question of time before he would apply himself to a study of the supreme Personality of the world's history. The opening paragraph strikes the keynote of the new book: 'From the very beginning of Our Lord's earthly life,' we read, 'there appears the substitution of the personal element for the purely legal element. He is a mysterious Personality and the whole success of His religion lies in its being trusted, followed, understood.'

The book is not a 'Life' of Christ—there are not a few such works on the market, some of them quite admirable. The Abbot's aim is not even directly devotional, in the narrow sense of that word. His book is a dogmatic treatise on the mystery of God made Man and on its tremendous consequences for mankind; but it is eminently 'edifying' in the original meaning of that lovely word coined by St Paul for describing the purpose and significance of every spiritual activity in the Church (*cf.* I Cor. xiv *passim*). The Abbot writes: 'Any man may invent an ascetical system and find others to submit to it, but no man can make of his own person the irrevocable voice of conscience, the all-satisfying food of heart and mind; Our Lord is the only Person

who ever could' (*Coll. Works*, I, 98). All this is profoundly true, for
Christ is the very embodiment of truth, the only way that leads to the
Father, the supreme manifestation in time of the invisible God who
inhabits eternity. The author is perhaps on less sure ground when he
asks whether the personal love of Christ, as history reveals it, might
not be taken as a pyschological proof of His divine reality. The wording
is somewhat vague and he does not answer his own query beyond
adding that 'one thing is certain: nothing like it [viz. love for Christ]
exists elsewhere; the personalities of non-Christian religions do not
enter into the human consciousness in the way that Christ does'
(*ibid.*, p. 99).

The Jubilee year of 1925 saw the publication of what was, undoubtedly, the Abbot's most weighty contribution to theological
thought. Very modestly he gave it the title of *A Key to the Doctrine of
the Eucharist*. If he had called it *The Key*, he would not have been pre-
sumptuous. His book is a golden key that unlocks the door to a whole
world of supernatural marvels, and to the forging of it the Abbot gave
the best that was in him. The book appeared at a most opportune
moment, for just about this time there had been much heated controversy about the nature of the Eucharistic sacrifice. It looked as if the key
to the mystery had been lost, or at least mislaid. The Abbot's book was
the fruit of prolonged pondering of the teaching of St Thomas and
is largely a paraphrase of the *Summa*, Pt. III, q. LXXIII ff. Abbot Vonier
was no Moses coming down from the heights of speculation with a
new revelation, and if some readers regarded his expounding of the
mystery as 'novel', their surprise was due to the fact that they, not the
Abbot, had forgotten or misinterpreted the traditional teaching of 'our
Masters'.

This is not the place to recall the controversies of three decades ago
as to what constitutes the sacrifice of the Mass. All Catholics hold that
the Mass is a true sacrifice, one that in its essentials is identical with the
bloody immolation of Calvary, but not all theologians account for
this identity in the same way. Abbot Vonier's contribution to the debate
was most effective because it was objective, calm and serene. He wisely
began his exposition with a study of sacramental significance and
efficacy. Since the Eucharist is a sacrament—*the* sacrament in fact—it
needs must be viewed in the light of sacramental theology.

A sacrament is by definition a sign, a token, hinting at, or pointing
to, a supernatural reality which precisely because it is supernatural does
not come within the range of the senses. Yet it is no *mere* sign; on the

contrary, it is effective of that which it signifies, though the energy in virtue of which it operates is ultimately derived from Christ; hence the sacrament is a true cause, though an instrumental one. 'The sacraments of the New Law,' says St Thomas, 'effect that which they signify.' This doctrine is also valid for the Eucharist. In this sacrament both words and actions signify, or point to Christ's body and blood, hence, if the above definition is valid—and we know it to be so from the authoritative teaching of the Church—the words of the priest effect, or produce the body and blood of Christ *sacramentally*, that is, not in their natural, physical state, but precisely in the unique manner of this sacrament. The Eucharist is essentially a sacrifice, or to use the Abbot's phrase, a sacramental sacrifice, for though the Victim is sacrificed, it is so, not in its natural state, but in the sacramental one. The whole significance of this sacrament bears a sacrificial character since *vi verborum*, that is, in virtue of the words spoken first by Christ and after Him by the priest, under the *species* of the bread there is only Christ's body, and under that of the wine we have only His blood, though in actual fact, in consequence of Our Lord's impassibility and utter immutability since His resurrection, there is no actual separation of body and blood, no 'mactation', as they say, in this unique sacrifice. The immediate effect of the words spoken over the bread and the wine is to change the bread into the body of Christ and the wine into His blood. This is the sacramental immolation, though by reason of 'natural concomitance' no real separation can take place in the risen Christ, either of body and blood or of these from His soul. Therefore, since the words of the two-fold consecration, which are the 'form' of the sacrament, 'effect what they signify' *and no more*, the natural physical immolation on the cross is presented anew in the sacramental immolation of every Mass.' The sacrifice of Calvary was a natural sacrifice, for Christ was then physically immolated. On the altar that sacrifice is re-enacted, evoked and made present in the same way as at the Last Supper, as St Paul learnt from Our Lord Himself (I Cor. xi. 23 f.); 'This do . . . for the commemoration of me . . . as often as you shall eat this bread and drink the chalice, you shall show forth the death of the Lord until He come.' A sacrament is no mere symbol—it effects, or contains that which it signifies—else it would not be a sacrament at all. It is on this basic notion that the Abbot built up the theology of the Eucharistic sacrifice—a sacramental sacrifice because the Victim is not offered and exhibited in its natural mode of existence, but under other forms, viz. the forms of bread and wine.

It must be admitted that for a full appreciation of a book such as this a certain familiarity with the method and the terminology of scholastic philosophy would be required. The popularity of the book was undoubtedly due, at least in part, to the fact that it provided an eminently satisfying alternative, not to say a corrective, for a view of the Eucharistic sacrifice put forward by a distinguished theologian which by some was hailed as a new revelation and by others denounced as trenching upon heresy. When we recall the heated controversies around Père de la Taille's monumental tome, *Mysterium Fidei*, we cannot but be impressed by the calm, measured, closely reasoned paragraphs in which Abbot Vonier expounds what he regarded as the traditional teaching of the Church. While one or two of the distinguished Jesuit's opponents were rushing to the defence of what they, like the Abbot, rightly regarded as the teaching of St Thomas and the Council of Trent, with a zeal akin to fierceness, ready, so it seemed, to gather inquisitorial faggots for an *auto-da-fé*, not indeed of the author, but at least of his book, Abbot Vonier judged that a calm, measured exposition of that teaching would carry far greater weight than a violent rebuttal of an opinion that is certainly not heretical even though it may seem to be at variance with the doctrine of the Angelic Doctor. Let the reader judge for himself: 'It is the very nature of the Eucharistic Sacrifice to be representative of the past, not a "mactation" (slaying) of the present. Christ's body and blood (on the altar) *represent*, aptly and completely, that phase of His earthly career when He was dead on the cross, they do not in any way represent . . . His glorious life in heaven. . . . His body and blood, separated in sacramental truth, can be the memory or representation of that Lord whose body was on the cross, whose blood was poured out on the hill of Calvary. . . . When Christ was body and blood only, He was the perfect sacrifice, and the Eucharist is a perfect sacrifice because it again makes present—such is the literal meaning of re-presentation—all that was on this earth of Christ after He had pronounced His *Consummatum est* . . .' (*Coll. Works*, II, 288).

This passage does not by any means give us a complete picture of the world of marvels that is the Eucharist—one of which is concomitance. 'The Body and Blood of Christ are not found in isolation, and in fact were not isolated at the Last Supper . . . the Sacrament of the Eucharist has a *concomitance*, a *cortège* of splendours. The Body and Blood of Christ on the Christian altar are perfectly identical with the Body and Blood in heaven' (*ibid.*, p. 330). But the Abbot begs his reader to be quite clear about one thing, viz. that this *cortège* of new splendours has nothing to do with the sacrament as such; the sacrament is only that which it signifies, and the signification is only of the Body and Blood. 'The term concomitance is of immense importance: it is the full justification, in particular, of modern Eucharistic devotion . . . in the first period of the Church, the mystery of the Eucharist is invariably spoken of in *sacramental* terms, whereas we tend to speak of it in *personal* terms.' Writing as a theologian the Abbot had to insist on the basic principle that in the Eucharist we are not dealing directly with the 'person' of Christ, but with the 'sacrament', that is, the flesh and blood of Christ which are there found in virtue of the power and significance of the words with which He Himself changed the substance of bread and wine into the substance and reality of His flesh and blood.

The *Key to the Doctrine of the Eucharist* has been translated into all the greater European languages. A French clerical Review, while speaking of it in highly eulogistic terms, points out that the Abbot's main idea—that of sacrament, sacrifice, sacramental sacrifice—is not new. The Review rates this book as the most coherent of all his works, while the French translator describes it as 'so profound and so free of pedantry', and adds 'this remarkable theologian, faithful to tradition, inspired by St Paul, whom he knew by heart, and by St Thomas . . . does not go in for polished sentences. His mind, enlightened by faith, is a live mind, the doctrine he expounds is alive, satisfying.'

From that great humanist, who was also a genuine scholar, Dr Burton, Bishop of Clifton, the Abbot received a short letter which gave him considerable satisfaction. Written in that wonderful handwriting for which the Bishop was famous, and couched in his own trenchant, forthright phraseology, the letter is an episcopal *Imprimatur* of a quite unusual kind. The italics are the Bishop's. It runs as follows:

'DEAR FR ABBOT,

I am abominably busy, but *must* thank you for showing up the two fallacies (*lies*) of Lépin (Fr De la Taille):

Lie 1. that *offerre* in Catholic (or even pagan) parlance is used as an expression meaning only to *present a victim for acceptance—v.* "Bellarmine, *De Missa*, Lib. I, c. 15".

Lie 2. that *mystic* excludes what is *real*, *tanquam aliquid oppositum*, and that the Mass is but an *imago sacrificii*, *quia peragitur sub signo*, "*Myst. Fidei*, p. 241".

✠ G. A. CLIFT.'

Most of our ancient cathedrals and abbey churches, whether still in use or only picturesque ruins, have one feature in common—the sanctuary is surrounded by a circle of chapels, one of which, and as a rule the largest and most beautiful of them all, is the Lady Chapel. Abbot Anscar's literary work is like a majestic temple reared to the glory of Christ our Lord. It was in the nature of things that to this noble edifice he would add, as it were, a Lady Chapel. This he did when he wrote a little masterpiece of less than fifty pages. *The Divine Motherhood* was written in the course of the year 1920 and in fulfilment of a vow made at a moment when, during the Great War, the very existence of the community was in jeopardy. So the little book is a thank-offering to the Guardian and Patroness of this her very own house. The pages of the little book glow with a controlled emotional warmth far more effective, it seems to me, than the most perfervid declamations that one may hear in some Italian church during the May devotions. But in the last paragraph even he must let his heart speak. The passage is so revealing of his tender yet manly love and admiration for her who is the glory of our race, that it may be quoted as a fitting conclusion of this very incomplete survey of Abbot Vonier's written work.

After a somewhat laboured and even awkward comparison of Mary's motherhood with an immense lake situated in the centre of an island surrounded by the immensity of the sea, viz. the Divine Word's eternal generation, he addresses her in these terms: 'From thee, as from a point of vantage, I hope to contemplate for ever the two Lives in which lies the happiness of all created intellects—the Life that is born in eternity and the Life that was born in time. There was a time when the world's evil frightened my soul; when I looked upon it with scared eyes and an anguished heart, as if it were something mighty with power and substance in it. But from the day when I began to understand thy motherhood more clearly, and to love it more ardently, my soul has ever made merry over the idle efforts of the princes of darkness to establish a mendacious sovereignty of gloom. The Creator of the starry skies smiles sweetly on thee, O fairest of all women, and thou returnest His smile in triumphant peace. I know that with God smiling at His sweet Mother the grim powers of evil are already defeated' (*Coll. Works*, I, 376).

What is the Abbot's place among the spiritual or theological writers of the first half of the present century? During his lifetime he had a vast company of admirers who welcomed every new book of his with enthusiasm. But wise old Horace's saying remains ever true:

habent sua fata libelli,

books have their day. None would agree more whole-heartedly than Abbot Vonier. How often one has heard him say that only a very few writers could hope to be read fifty years hence. All we can do is to speak to our contemporaries. It is a writer's duty to keep the debate going. The only originality that is possible at this date is the personal note which a sincere writer is bound to strike when in his turn he lays before his contemporaries the result of his reflections upon the eternal, unchanging verities. Of this kind is Abbot Vonier's originality. I think it is safe to say that he was unlike any other writer of his time—he spoke a language, and in accents all his own. Most of the others probably wrote much more elegantly, but none more vigorously. He cannot be classed with those of his contemporaries who were theologians *ex professo* and, apparently, had no other tasks on their hands. Nor is he another Marmion, though both men, in the words of Scripture, had for their supreme aim 'to strengthen godliness in the days of sinners' (Ecclus. xlix. 4), an aim which both knew could only be attained if piety was solidly founded on sound doctrine. Both men, moreover, had this in common that they wrote and spoke in an idiom they had not learnt at their mother's knee.

Abbot Vonier's literary work has not escaped criticism—not only on the heading of style, but, what is more serious, on that of the presentation of his subject-matter. It has been said that 'he was a robust rather than a subtle thinker' and that 'he saw large outlines and general views, but his perception of detail and fine shades of distinction was not so deep'. But it is precisely the massiveness of his thought, the vigour with which he formulates it and his refusal to be diverted from his main point by a mass of secondary issues which are such distinctive characteristics of his work, that appealed to a large public who time and again expressed their gratitude and testified to the profit they derived from the solid spiritual and intellectual food provided by his books. The Abbot's aim in taking up his pen was a purely apostolic one, viz. that of opening the eyes of educated men and women to the splendours of the Catholic faith. His writing was supplementary to his oral teaching, for he was an indefatigable preacher. Such being his purpose he had no need of a learned apparatus, of serried ranks of footnotes, or numerous quotations and references to writers known or obscure. He loved a large canvas and painted with bold strokes and vivid colours, but it does not follow that the small detail escaped him. It simply did not suit his purpose to busy himself with secondary or accessory questions. As a matter of fact, large outlines and broad views were outstanding features of all his undertakings.

A famous nineteenth-century bishop once said that if St Paul were to return to earth he would run a newspaper. In our own days we might go further and say that, besides his epistles, he would also write a few novels, for at this time, if a man thinks he has a message for humanity, or is bent on spreading an idea, redressing a wrong, or defending a right, he uses the press and, as often as not, writes a novel.

Strange as it must seem to those who only knew him from his books, or for having heard him preach, the Abbot long toyed with the idea of writing a novel—a doctrinal, theological novel—which seems a contradiction in terms. Knowing that the readers of serious books are few, whereas everybody reads fiction, he wished to make use of this medium to spread the faith. He spoke of this project repeatedly. One summer's evening, towards the end of a long afternoon spent on the hills that rise behind Buckfast, he and I stood for a while near the rustic gate by which we had entered the enchanting world of Dartmoor. Silently we were contemplating the lovely panorama of fields and meadows, hills and valleys spread before our eyes in the golden light of the westering sun. Here and there blue smoke rose from the chimneys of isolated farmhouses—as in the haunting last lines of the first eclogue:

Iamque summa procul villarum culmina fumant,

when he suddenly spoke and asked: 'How can we bring the Catholic faith to the people who live here, in this little earthly paradise? I think I must write a novel—a novel full of doctrine.' I am afraid he was disappointed by my lack of enthusiasm for his notion. I felt that with all his ability he was ill-equipped for such an undertaking. The training of a monk, or for that matter, of an ecclesiastic, does not prepare him for this type of literary activity. There can be little doubt that had the Abbot made the attempt his would have been a very bad novel—as a novel—whatever might have been its merits as an exposition of Catholic belief and practice.

CHAPTER XI

THE PREACHER

DURING Abbot Vonier's lifetime every new book of his never failed to meet with a warm and even enthusiastic welcome from a very considerable body of readers. It must be frankly admitted that this popularity was not so much due to any outstanding literary quality of his work, if we view it solely as literature. In this respect some of his output leaves much to be desired. But when this is granted I must add at once that any stylistic blemishes are readily condoned, in fact are scarcely noticed, by the serious reader engrossed, as he soon becomes, in the limpid, illuminating and profoundly satisfying presentation of whatever subject the Abbot may be treating. The dead are soon forgotten; so are their achievements. In our days the printing-press churns out, year by year, an ever-growing mass of reading matter, both religious and profane, yet Abbot Vonier's books continue to be in demand though he has been dead these eighteen years. There could be no more solid proof of their intrinsic worth since it is a fact that most people tend to take up the latest book almost before the ink is dry on its pages, rather than one by a writer who, for so many, is now little more than a name. The Abbot himself derived intense satisfaction from his literary success, not, indeed, because he courted popularity, but because he realized that by means of his books he could exercise a most beneficent influence upon the spiritual and intellectual life of thousands whose souls he would not be able to contact by any other means.

For all that, and great as is the value of his writings, I think it is as a preacher and lecturer that he was at his best and made the strongest impact both upon his immediate religious family and upon his contemporaries in general. For one thing, he was a born teacher, for, as was said in the previous chapter, he had not only wide learning and a strong, vital grasp of the things of the spirit, but he also possessed a remarkable ability to impart his knowledge to others—a gift not invariably enjoyed by the learned—even to people whom we take it upon ourselves to describe as uneducated for the sole reason that they have not had the educational facilities that we ourselves may have had. The Abbot thoroughly enjoyed lecturing and preaching. Sunday after Sunday, year in and year out, during the whole period of his abbacy, he occupied the pulpit of the Abbey church, while many, if not most, of his absences from home were due to some preaching engagement elsewhere. He took an utterly supernatural view of what St Peter calls 'the ministry of the word', while his faith in the power of the spoken word was unlimited. In a letter to the Abbess of Dourgne, written at the beginning of 1910, there occurs a revealing autobiographical passage: 'I believe,' he writes, 'that I might have become a popular preacher in one of the European languages if the habit of weighing and measuring all things, even those belonging to the spiritual and ascetical life, had not clipped my wings.'

By this time he was already in considerable demand as a special preacher on important occasions and he also preached in some of the London churches. From the first his public utterances were remarkable by reason of the fervour and earnestness with which he spoke. In the first period of what we may call his public life he was the victim—I think that is the right word—of a kind of infatuation with the writings of Thomas Carlyle. One may well wonder how many people could truthfully affirm that they had ploughed through the vast output of the cantankerous philosopher of Chelsea. The future Abbot of Buckfast was one such brave spirit; with the result that, for a while, he would quote Carlyle both frequently and with obvious relish. This was matter for mild amusement for most of the community, but it ended by exasperating the late Fr Savinian Louismet, a simple and devout man and the author of several little books on mysticism which had a great vogue during his lifetime but which by now probably gather dust on the less accessible shelves of many a library. So there came a day when the good man felt he could no longer stand Carlyle in the pulpit, and since he was acting as assistant to the parish priest, the opportunity was ready to his hand. Accordingly, one Sunday evening, there came a moment in his sermon when he felt the need of quoting some authority to lend weight to what he was saying. By an apparent, but carefully calculated slip of the tongue, he said: 'Carlyle says—ah! no, my brethren,' he corrected himself, 'not Carlyle—Carlyle was not a Father of the Church—St Augustine says . . .'. What the great African was reputed to have said I cannot now recollect, but I do remember that, like Queen Victoria on a different occasion, the Abbot, Dom Boniface Natter, was not amused. However, from this time forward

Dom Anscar's sermons were no longer embellished by quotations from the works of Thomas Carlyle.

Like many a public speaker Dom Anscar had no other teacher than personal experience for, incredible though it now seems, no special training was given to the young priests, so that one had to learn the craft of preaching the hard way, by trial and error. In his case the process proved highly successful, so true it is that *orando fit orator*—by dint of speaking a man becomes an orator. In those early years there were those who thought they detected a certain *hauteur* in Dom Anscar's tone and manner, and in the village there were some who spoke of him as 'the proud monk'. In this judgment they were profoundly mistaken—the seeming aloofness of the young priest, the firm, dogmatic, one might say authoritative tone he adopted, were undoubtedly due to a certain nervousness, perhaps also to a measure of uneasiness due to the fact that he was speaking in a language he had only recently acquired and not yet completely mastered, but most of all to the circumstance that he was a young monk who, up till that time, had had scarcely any contacts with the outside world. Hence it was not surprising that he should address a very mixed audience more or less in the same strain as when he taught his students, or instructed the novices. However, his discourses were characterized by a freshness, an originality, a doctrinal solidity that compelled attention. The voice may have been harsh, the foreign accent strongly marked, the delivery and accompanying gestures by no means in strict conformity with the manuals devised for the guidance of public speakers—but here was a man with a message, who knew he had a message, and who was determined to deliver it. At this time the community of Buckfast was exceedingly small, hence Dom Anscar had perforce to play many rôles, including the seemingly irreconcilable ones of cellarer and professor of theology. In March 1905 he wrote to his sister, a nun of the Assumption in Paris, where she discharged lowly and exacting duties in the kitchen of a large convent: 'You need not ask for news of me: my days are spent like yours, though not in the kitchen to which, however, I repair occasionally in my capacity of cellarer—but in a variety of occupations, from the teaching of lofty theology to the care of cows and pigs. In my cell things are strangely jumbled together—ledgers jostle with treatises on metaphysics, and business letters with sermon manuscripts, memorandums on the price of split peas and sugar with philosophical theses. All this shows you the intellectual chaos in which I live—*dans quelle cuisine intellectuelle je vis.*' The correspondence was in French.

Over a number of years Buckfast was frequently called upon to send priests to Dartmoor Prison, to enable the chaplain to go on leave, or to replace him during his not infrequent bouts of illness. This work was extremely popular with the Fathers, and anyone who had once ministered to the occupants of the grim halls known to tens of thousands of tourists and holiday-makers, was always eager to go back, for everyone felt that here was a unique opportunity to bring comfort to the souls of the unhappy men who, to be sure, had been at loggerheads with the law of God and man, but who often enough were also little more than victims of adverse circumstances and the lack of a wholesome social background. Dom Anscar quickly won the respect and confidence of the men 'staying on the Moor', very much against their will. He also became most acceptable to the prison authorities; in fact, a strong and lasting friendship between him and the governor, Mr. Basil Thomson as he then was, was forged at that time, a friendship that was to stand us in good stead in 1914, as the reader will remember, when thanks to Sir Basil's intervention, the German nationals of the Abbey—and they formed the majority of the community—were exempted from the general internment of all 'enemy' aliens.

It was in the Catholic chapel of Dartmoor Prison that Dom Anscar preached his first mission. It is no small advantage for a young priest to start mission work in a prison—the inexperienced missionary is at least sure of a congregation. On this occasion, in the autumn of 1904, Dom Anscar appealed to his sister for spiritual help, for his trust in the power of her prayers was unbounded. On 1st November he wrote: 'The feast of today [All Saints] makes me think of you; but even more so my present need. I am in prison, not for any misdeed, but in order to do some good to my friends here—burglars, thieves, murderers, and what not. On Sunday, 6th of this month, I am to begin a regular mission which will go on for a whole week. You know what this means for you. *I* shall be preaching the mission more or less well—rather less well, in fact, but as for grace and conversions, that is *your* affair. I'll let you know later on what success your efforts shall have achieved. If the mission is a failure, you will have to bear the shame of it. This intention—and many others—are of infinitely greater importance than mutual condolences over temporary, or temporal disasters [the reference is to the persecution and expulsion of religious communities in France at that time]. Do not imagine that the empire of Jesus Christ will collapse for so little. If you have influence with Him, you can laugh hell and its minions to scorn. The real enemy is unfaithfulness to His love. I really care very little where you may be sent to. This earth is so small that I cannot understand why we talk of distance. What do I care whether I live in Indo-China or at Timbuctoo? There too I shall always be myself and not an inch nearer to, or farther from, Our Lord. There are distances of a far more alarming nature—those are the ones I fear. As for souls—you find them everywhere and they are all of them cast in the same mould. In any case, your duty at the moment is not to complain on account of M. Combes, to whom I wish paradise at the end of his days, but to make sure that I have a successful mission to my convicts, three hundred of them: you see you have your work cut out for you.'

He had promised to report on the mission. He did so in a second letter, dated 16th November: 'I have to thank you,' he wrote, 'for all you have done to make the mission a success. Much good has been done. . . . I return to the monastery with a burning conviction that prayer and sacrifice are indispensable conditions for the salvation of souls. Let us be prepared for persecution, even unto death, so that, won by our fidelity, Our Lord may be moved to pity, were it only towards one single soul, and so receive it into his peace. He is the Sun of right-eousness; from Him all light derives; where no ray of His brightness penetrates all is darkness. It is within your power to induce Him to flash ever more powerful shafts of light into the chaos of souls.'

This letter, one of a large number written over a period of forty years, is indicative of the lofty and utterly supernatural view he took of his apostolic activities—as, in fact, he did of all his enterprises. In every one of his letters to his sister we meet with an ever recurrent request for prayers and vivid expressions of his sincere conviction that whatever good he was able to do was her work. When he spoke thus he was utterly sincere. He would be the last man to indulge in the pious *clichés* so soothing for certain pious ears and often current in religious circles because they are deemed appropriate and edifying. In another letter written at a later date, after a retreat given to the community of Buckfast by Abbot Oswald Smith of Ampleforth, whom Abbot Vonier described as 'a real saint', he tells his sister that the Abbot of Ampleforth had spoken of a distinguished priest who enjoyed great popularity and whose every enterprise seemed to prosper. When con-gratulated upon his success that good priest was wont to say that it was all due to the prayers of a holy sister of his. 'That is also my case,' Abbot Vonier declared. 'I too have a sister who is responsible for whatever success I achieve.'

8

Small wonder then, that when in 1911 he was invited to preach a course of sermons at the twelve o'clock Mass at Westminster Cathedral his first thought was to enlist the help of Sister Swithbert. He was obviously highly gratified by the invitation—for one thing his appearance in that pulpit, before the vast and varied crowd that makes up the congregation of that Mass, could hardly fail to draw attention to his building operations at Buckfast and, maybe, would win new benefactors. But above all he was profoundly conscious of the extraordinary importance of his task. 'I was about to write,' he told his sister, 'in order to recommend to you a very big affair. Next Sunday I enter upon my career as a preacher to the great world—*le grand monde*. No! I beg your pardon, this is not what I meant to say. What I mean is that I am to give a course of sermons in the vast cathedral of Westminster. Obtain for me the grace that I may only seek Our Lord's glory. You will be with me in spirit.'

His discourses made a profound impression. On each of the four Sundays of the course the vast building was filled to capacity. Thereafter he preached repeatedly both in the Cathedral and in some of the big London churches. The general impression was that here was a preacher with a difference. As I have said already, he lacked not a few of the qualifications demanded by the treatises on the art of public speaking. His English, though grammatically correct, lacked polish and real distinction. He never had a lesson in voice production, hence his voice was not invariably well modulated, in fact—it could be harsh when he got excited; the foreign accent was very marked, and the gestures—fortunately he was not greatly addicted to them—were often awkward; but there was a light in his eyes, an earnestness in his tone, an indefinable something in his whole person—otherworldliness perhaps is the best word for it—that gripped the listeners and held their attention. Above all it was the profound truths, the majestic dogmas of Christianity, man's high destiny and his sublime hopes, expounded with a clarity and a simplicity amounting to genius, that captivated minds and hearts and so enthralled the hearers that whatever defects there may have been in the delivery passed almost unnoticed or, in actual fact, rather added to the effectiveness of his discourses.

Abbot Vonier was a preacher who honoured the intelligence of the average Christian man and woman. Very properly he deemed 'the ordinary man or woman' perfectly capable of grasping, or at least of appreciating, the highest doctrines of the Christian faith; all that was needed was to put these solemn truths before them stripped of the technical terminology of the lecture-room. How often he would urge his own priests to 'preach theology, the people have a right to have it expounded to them'. Here was the real secret of his great popularity—he gave the Christian people what they wanted—solid, substantial doctrine. In his book *The People of God* (*Coll. Works*, II, 207) he writes: 'It is a great gain towards our understanding of the Christian mysteries when we are willing to look upon them as being instituted, not for an *élite*, but for a people.' This holds good in the doctrinal sphere. There can be no esoteric element in a revelation made by God for the benefit of all mankind. St Paul's sublimest epistles, those in which he treats of the most recondite mysteries of our faith, were written for the instruction of very ordinary folk, for surely the 'saints' of Ephesus, Philippi or Collossae did not greatly differ from the good, faithful people who flock to our churches Sunday after Sunday. Hence our people are entitled to have the loftiest or, if you like, the deepest truths of religion expounded to them. In point of fact I would even make bold to maintain that the twenty-centuries-old tradition of Christian faith and practice, of which the present-day Catholics are the heirs, enables them to grasp these great truths more readily than did the men and women of long ago, as they listened to St Paul's letters when they were read to them when they came together in church upon the Lord's day. Abbot Vonier was undoubtedly inspired by this idea throughout his life. 'Any exclusiveness in the distribution of the good things of Christianity,' he wrote, 'is an abomination in the eyes of God. . . . Christ and His religion are not for the privileged classes but for the masses . . . it is the higher life of a whole people' (*ibid.*, p. 208).

But for all his love of the ordinary people, and in spite of his own opinion (as stated in a letter to the Abbess of Dourgne already quoted), it is most unlikely that he could ever have become a 'popular preacher', precisely by reason of his life within the shelter of the cloister. The monastic life is a sheltered life, hence contacts with the workaday world are of necessity no more than incidents for a monk, and his acquaintance with life in the raw is at best only second-hand. For all that it would have been a strange thing if one whose insight into the things of the spirit was so clear and so vivid should have been unable to clothe his thoughts in language and imagery that would be within the grasp of people of average intelligence and education. Whatever criticism may have been passed on his teaching, I cannot recollect anyone ever complaining that he spoke 'above people's heads'. He carefully eschewed difficult words, and if a technical term could not be dispensed with he was at pains to explain its meaning.

That he could adapt himself to any audience is proved by the fact that he was asked to address the most diverse gatherings. One sample of this enviable gift must suffice—it is taken from a talk on the Mass addressed to Catholic schoolgirls and shows with what delightful simplicity he could expound the wealth and splendour of the Mass. His very first sentence was calculated to awaken interest and to capture the imagination of modern children, for how could they fail to be interested in the picture of a big ship? 'One of the wonders of our civilization,' he told his youthful audience, 'are the ships that cross the seas of the world. The *Queen Mary* does the trip between England and America in less than one hundred hours, just about the time of an ordinary school-retreat. But though she is colossal, she is not formidable: on the contrary, she is the most gracious thing afloat, in which children, and even babes in arms, will cross the terrible Atlantic with as much confidence as if they were in their own country. No doubt she will carry big men, big not in size but in importance—statesmen and learned men—but such weight will not make any difference. . . . This seems to me a not inappropriate simile for the great mystery of the Mass. In that most divine contrivance for taking souls to heaven, the big and the small, the learned and the unlearned, the saints and the sinners are equally at home—they are all of them carried forward on the ocean of Christ's Blood, through the power of Christ's charity. When we are at Mass we ought to realize . . . that we are passengers to heaven in God's own ship. He designed it for us. He built it for us, He even places us in it—and above all, we have a free passage. . . . Mass is a great mystery which does all its work independently of us, our share being just this that we are *in* it. The holiest and most learned of men, when at Mass, cannot do anything more exalted than just to know that they are in the very midst of a divine mystery.' He then pointed out that 'the passengers are not expected to help in the running of the ship—it is enough that they remain in it: thus, when at Mass, all we need do is to reap its benefits. Even when we say our own prayers and have our own devotions at Mass, we do what the passengers on the liner do when they take the air on deck. . . . Christ, the Son of God, does everything, the beatings of His Heart are the only true activities of the Mass.

'There is no ship without its crew—"the ship's company", as it is called—so are we in a marvellous company while at Mass. If we read the Canon of the Mass we cannot but be surprised at the repeated allusions to the company of the elect . . . we speak to Peter, Paul, Andrew and James . . . we are in touch with John and Stephen, Matthias and Barnabas, Agatha, Lucy and Agnes . . . nor does the Canon exclude any saint of any age. So while we are at Mass we may most legitimately feel that we are the travelling-companions of the elect in heaven and of all good and holy people on earth. The Mass is the greatest social function in the Kingdom of Christ.'

All this is charming and apparently effortless. However, the Abbot was undoubtedly more at home with grown-ups. There exists a large number of sermons and addresses of his in typescript. They are of very uneven value, though in every one of them there is a solid kernel, a thought, or an aspect of truth that could not fail to make an impression on an earnest listener. There were occasions when his approach to his subject was perhaps painfully slow and laboured; it almost looked as if he needed warming up—like the engine of a car that has stood in the open through a chilly night. It was even said that at times he preached one and a half sermons! The occasion for this remark was the fact that, as he spoke Sunday after Sunday, he frequently summed up what he had said on the previous Sunday before coming to his chosen subject. This procedure could be tiresome, and of course, added not a little to the time he spent in the pulpit.

It is in the nature of things that his best public utterances were those which he had not merely carefully thought out, but which he had likewise written in his own hand. However, he was not the man to stick slavishly to a manuscript. Like every genuine orator, as distinct from a mere speaker who talks because he must, Abbot Vonier was strongly influenced both by the occasion, the place and the audience. While he was giving his first course of sermons at Westminster Cathedral, he made a point of attending the crowded High Mass which preceded the midday Mass at which he was to preach. This he did—as he explained—in order to work himself into an appropriate frame of mind; the sight of so many people, all of them of one mind and heart, seemed to expand his own mind and to help him to cast his ideas, as it were, into a larger mould. Extensive quotations alone would show how successful this policy was, but a few extracts from one or two of his very latest public utterances must suffice. In the last years, nay, the last months of his life, when worn out, and walking, though he knew it not, in the daily thickening shadow of death, he was intellectually at the height of his powers. By that time too he spoke with the authority that age and experience alone can bestow on a man. One of these final utterances was addressed to a large gathering of the members of the *Catholic Evidence Guild*. To these lay-apostles of both sexes he propounded a profound truth, one that cannot be too often, or too forcefully stressed, namely, that 'it is the mission of a herald of Catholic truth never to separate the twin notions of the Kingdom of God and the Personality of Christ'. 'On this point,' he said, 'we differ profoundly from the humanitarians on the one hand, and from the evangelicals and the pietists on the other.'

'It would be a comparatively easy task,' he told his audience, 'at least in England, to make the name of Christ popular. We have round about us enough of the remnants of traditional protestantism which does not hesitate to make capital out of the Name of Jesus. We have the Salvation Army doing it; we have a variety of sects still glorying in the Name; we have societies of Christian colportage plastering walls and fences with fiery texts and exhorting people to have faith in Jesus. Why is it that we Catholics cannot do these blatant things? Perhaps sometimes we think we ought to do them, that we ought to make a bolder proclamation of our faith in the Son of God. But we feel instinctively—and in this we are quite right—that it would be treason to Catholicism if we presented to the world a Christ in a state of isolation, detached from His Kingdom, separated from the Church with which He has surrounded Himself. . . .

'Belief in Christ's divinity is not everything—you have also to submit to that mystery of grace which is the Church, with her sacraments. . . . Protestantism, whose mentality surrounds us on all sides like a vapour, has not erred gravely in the matter of Christ's Personality, but it has erred gravely in the matter of the Kingdom of God. . . . Institutional Christianity, in other words, the Kingdom of God, is the only true home of the Son of God. . . .'

A public speaker's first aim is to please his hearers so as to win their sympathy for what he has to put before them. Time was when men delighted in the accessories of eloquence—the music of words, the charm of a voice, the grace of gesture and attitude. At this day these things leave us cold and the very word 'rhetoric' bears a pejorative connotation. That which ultimately impresses the modern man and rouses him to action is the content, the inner kernel, in other words, the objectivity of what he hears, joined to the sincerity of the speaker, hence a man may be a persuasive speaker and yet lack not a few of the graces of eloquence. Deep earnestness was the outstanding characteristic

of Abbot Vonier's public utterances. I have no hesitation in assert-
ing that, whatever the occasion, Abbot Vonier never rose to speak
merely because he was expected to do so. Whenever he spoke he had
something to say. Even though there were occasions when he churned
out words laboriously, or took time to come to the point, he never
failed to give utterance to a thought that would somehow strike home
and set the hearers thinking. On his lips even an after-dinner speech
sounded like a Church Father's homily and might have been delivered
with equal propriety at the Pontifical High Mass which usually preceded the repast that provided the occasion for this kind of oratory.

As I have said, we have at Buckfast a considerable quantity of
sermon matter of the Abbot's, but, with few exceptions, none of these
discourses and conferences is fully worked out, hence there can be no
question of their publication. The explanation is that he was wont to
speak extempore. He never read his discourses, except on rare and formal occasions, as when he lectured at a summer-school or at similar
gatherings.

The Abbot's last public appearance in this country was on 30th
October 1938, less than two months before his death, in St George's
Hall, Liverpool, the occasion being one of those great rallies which
Archbishop Downey was wont to hold annually for the purpose of
fostering enthusiasm for his grandiose scheme for a cathedral that
would only be second in size to St Peter's in Rome. The Archbishop
cherished a warm friendship for the Abbot and greatly admired him,
not only as a theologian, but for his architectural achievement at Buckfast. He rightly felt that the mere appearance on the platform of one
who had accomplished so much with such slender resources would
make a powerful appeal to the imagination of the ardent Catholics of
Liverpool. When he introduced the Abbot to the vast audience, the
Archbishop described him as a man of world renown, a man of vision,
one in the great tradition of the medieval cathedral builders, who saw
what could be done with the blessing of God and who had the determination and perseverance to do it.

The Abbot's address roused the listeners to great enthusiasm.
Though delivered in a secular hall, it could have been spoken with
perfect propriety in the nearby pro-cathedral, a structure which, by
reason of its small dimensions and utter inadequateness as a cathedral,
is by itself a most eloquent appeal for a worthier metropolitan church.
When he spoke at Liverpool the Abbot was on his way to Rome, so his
address in St George's Hall was his last public utterance in this country.

Everybody knows that the most soul-stirring discourse loses much of its appeal when reproduced in cold print, yet even after the lapse of close on twenty years, Abbot Vonier's words that night have lost none of their actuality and urgency. With his very first sentence he raised the whole subject to the supernatural sphere—a sphere to which an undertaking such as that to which Dr Downey had set his hand, by right belongs. 'The building of your cathedral,' the Abbot told the enthusiastic crowd, 'is like all Christian life, a contact with Christ. . . . Your work on the cathedral is a deed done to the Body of Christ. The Son of God, I make bold to say, listens to every hammer-blow whilst this temple rises day by day, and His Sacred Heart rejoices because it is a canticle to Him of His loving people. But it is more than a song of praise—it is a war-song, it is a battle-cry, because with this mighty work you challenge the world's infidelity, you prove yourselves to be builders of God's stronghold.'

Some of his remarks in the course of this address, delivered, let it be noted, just one month short of a year before the outbreak of Hitler's war, seem to strike an almost prophetic note. 'There is no doubt in my mind,' he said, 'and an increasing number of men feel it in their innermost being—that we are up against very dark powers. . . . There are at work human, anyhow created intelligences, who think darkly and who are determined to impose on mankind their own mode of thought. . . . Forces are advancing, imbued with a fiery enthusiasm, for whom liberty is nothing, for whom fierce hatred of Christian freedom is the very breath of their nostrils. There is in this war of ideologies an element which only the blind cannot see—it is a striving for a supremacy opposed to the supremacy of God. We have not quite arrived at the point where, in the words of St Paul, "a man will show himself in the temple of God as if he were God", but we are in the thick of that apostasy which makes man consider himself as the last end of all things.' He then recounted an experience of his youth—how, when he began to study St Paul, he found it difficult to take his words literally, but that now he experienced no such reluctance. 'Modern civilization,' he said, 'has so exaggerated the value and rôle of man, has so completely banished God from human affairs, that it may be quite easy, one day, for a man to represent himself as a kind of incarnation of humanism, as the head of the race, as its god.'

The purpose of the rally was to raise funds for the gigantic task on which the Archbishop had embarked. However, Abbot Vonier made no formal appeal for money. Since the cathedral was a protest against modern infidelity, a challenge to the tyrants of the hour on the continent of Europe, and a profession of loyalty to Christ the King, he felt there was no need to mention gold or silver. He was content to impress upon his audience the fact that their Archbishop was doing them the honour of regarding them as the genuine successors of the great Christian generations of the past who built the great abbeys and cathedrals which are still the objects of our admiration. 'Above all the Archbishop has made it possible for every one of you—by joining in this great work—to proclaim before the world that in these terrible days of Antichrist there is burning within you a fierce fire, an undimmed flame—your love for Christ the King.'

From Liverpool the Abbot journeyed to France, for the purpose of giving the community retreat at the ancient abbey of St Martin of Ligugé, founded by St Martin himself. On 11th November, in that venerable church, he preached the panegyric of the great wonder-worker of the West. At Ligugé the Abbot had an audience well able to appreciate what he had to give—and he gave of his very best to that cultivated, highly disciplined body of men. A paragraph of *La Vie Bénédictine*, a periodical published by the Monks of Ligugé, subsequently described him as 'a linguist acquainted with all the fine points of the French language, who knew how to adjust it to the spontaneous sallies of English humour, thereby tempering in a most delicate fashion what by reason of the loftiness of his doctrine might have proved too sustained a strain.' The theme of the retreat was 'The Kingdom of God'. Of the panegyric of St Martin the same periodical remarked that 'by reason of its spiritual import and its actuality it was incomparably more than a mere feat of eloquence.'

Those were the days of the fantastic triumphs of that sinister triumvirate, Stalin, Hitler and Mussolini, when at least the first two 'spoke great words', as the prophet Daniel expresses it (vii. 8). The preacher accordingly recounted the famous incident in St Martin's life when Satan showed himself to the saint in the gaudy trappings of royalty, claiming that he was the Christ. 'I will not believe in the advent of Christ unless He bear the same aspect as on the day of His Passion, unless He shows me the wounds of His cross,' the saint protested. Like St Paul, Martin would only glory in the cross of Christ (Gal. vi. 14).

'Today,' the Abbot said, 'we behold on every side the terrifying spectacle of religious ideals, mysticisms, philosophies of life which will have none of Christ. Leaving on one side Red atheism, we have to consider certain deisms, all of them within an ace of pantheism, as the real danger of our time and the most tremendous preparation for the advent of Antichrist. . . . Eighteenth-century European deism was an attempt at religion without Christ; it led the world to the "Rights of Man" and the Revolution. Today, outside the confines of Soviet Russia, atheism does not run. But we may ask, is Europe's case any better on that account? I greatly fear that it is not. The appeals made to the deity are antichristian, complete negations of the Son of God. . . . Whatever the nature of the deity of which the leaders of contemporary racialism claim to be the chosen instruments, it is a deity in open opposition to Christ and His gospel.'

For all that, the Abbot remained an optimist, and, indeed, a Christian has no right to be a pessimist or to cherish defeatist notions. 'Christ's power abides in us,' the Abbot said; 'unfortunately it is only too true that Christians today, like Martin in his youth, hold commissions in the armies of Julian the Apostate. We are obliged to share in every phase—social, economic, political—of modern life, whose leaders and chiefs are so often apostates. We fain would get out of it all.' In a final reference to Satan's attempt to deceive Martin, the preacher declared that Christianity is now going through a similar experience. 'Are we not overawed by the sight of the masses seduced by self-styled saviours of society who openly boast . . . that they have succeeded where Christianity has failed?' Yet even he, confirmed optimist though he was, evidently found it hard to preserve his equanimity in the gathering gloom of the last months that preceded the cataclysm of the Second World War. His concluding words are most revealing: 'Frankly,' he admitted 'it is not easy, without a strong act of faith, to see the infinite superiority of a Saviour who saves by the cross over the "saviours" who promise immediate redress. Their success of an hour adorns their brow with a diadem of gold; the crowds fall down before them in worship, "they will seduce many".' He concludes with a moving invocation of the great Wonder-worker: 'O Martin, blessed Pontiff, obtain for us the grace, in these days of Antichrist, like you to prefer the stigmata of Christ crucified to the false glitter of a civilization that has become utterly humanitarian.'

Abbot Vonier had for his contemporaries several noteworthy preachers—men like Bishop Hedley, Bede Jarrett, Vincent McNabb, Fr Martindale, Archbishop Goodier—while in the last two decades of his life Mgr Knox had already become a shining luminary in the ecclesiastical firmament. All these have published some of their sermons in book form, or made books out of sermon material. Abbot

Vonier did not follow this precedent and the decision was a wise one. With rare exceptions a sermon in print is like decantered wine that has been kept too long on the sideboard. The countless *imponderabilia*—the mood of the audience, the solemnity of the occasion, the subtle influence of the speaker's personality, the tone of his voice, the flash of his eye—all this is missing in the printed page. No doubt there are exceptions. As long as English or French is spoken, Newman and Bossuet will be read with pleasure and profit, but these two great men constitute a category by themselves. How, then, does Abbot Vonier compare with the pulpit orators I have enumerated? It is not for me to allocate to him his proper place in that distinguished gallery, but I think it is safe to say that as regards essentials, viz. originality, depth, freshness of thought and lucidity in its exposition, the Abbot of Buck-fast not only yields to none, but is not excelled by any one of them. In respect to accessories, however, viz. elegance and polish of style and literary graces, he compares unfavourably with his contemporaries. This is not surprising in view of the fact that English was not his native idiom, and though he used it with remarkable skill and singular felicity, it could scarcely be expected that he would handle so rich and highly developed an instrument with the sensitiveness and ease of those who had used none other from their earliest years. However, an out-standing preacher he was, and in many respects it may be said that there was no one quite like him.

A contributing cause of his popularity was his personality—he was a big man both physically and intellectually. Added to this was the circumstance that he presented himself to the world as a prelate of the Church, the head of a historic abbey, a man who had dared put his hand to an unheard-of enterprise and who was actually realizing it with brilliant success. Hence, even if at times he failed to rise to any great height, his very personality seemed to give weight to what he said, while no one could fail to sense, and to respond to, the tremendous earnestness of the speaker. Earnestness was the outstanding character-istic of the Abbot's preaching and teaching, combined with a seeming Olympian calm and imperturbability, though this did not by any means exclude a warmth and, at times, a tenderness of feeling which betrayed themselves in the softness of his voice and the gentleness of his accents. *Verba volant!* It is of the essence of speech that its effect is meant to be immediate, hence, in a sense, transient. That is why St Peter de-clared that the ministry of the word is the second essential duty of an apostle, prayer taking the first place. The man who is able to expound the same truths over and over again, year after year, while keeping the listeners' interest alive, is a great preacher. Abbot Vonier was such a man. This chapter may suitably conclude with two quotations, one a tribute from an unusually gifted lady and the other from an archbishop.

'In the summer of 1913 I was groping my way from unbelief towards the Catholic Church. I had realized that for me it was that or nothing; but the difficulties were great. Then I met with Abbot Vonier's newly published book *The Human Soul*. This cleared the ground for me, explaining almost everything that had seemed puzzling or unreasonable. It now appeared to me most probable that Christianity, and so Catholicism, was truth. But I could not stake my life on a high degree of probability. I could only wait, and pray as best I could for light.

'Then, on 22nd January 1914, I went to hear Abbot Vonier preach at Warwick Street. The impression of *power* was something the like of which I have never experienced before or since: the black-robed monk, with pale face and dark, flashing eyes, standing on the altar steps (there being no pulpit in that church); the foreign accent of a man mastering a language which was not his own, all enhanced the effect of what he said. And that, instead of being, as one so often feels, the careful working out of everything the preacher can say on his subject, was so condensed as to be difficult to follow. Almost every sentence might have been expanded into a sermon, and one was in danger of trying to follow a train of thought suggested by what he was saying at one moment and so missing what came next. He was no doubt working at *The Personality of Christ* at the time, for I afterwards recognized the substance of the sermon in Chapter XXX, "The Character of Christ".

'At the end I felt that something was breaking down—or opening out—within me; and when the monstrance was placed on the throne, I *knew*, with that incommunicable, almost imperceptible touch in the depths of one's being which is Faith. My *credo* was said, and I understood that if I ever went back on that, no matter what difficulties there might be, it would be the sin of infidelity.'

Writing in *The Tablet*, a couple of months after Abbot Vonier's death, Archbishop Mathew spoke of him in terms which it is all the more agreeable to quote here as they confirm the opinion expressed in this chapter, namely, that the Abbot was essentially an orator and at his very best when preaching and lecturing. 'Abbot Vonier', Dr Mathew wrote, 'was before all else a preacher and, when he came at

length to the full possession of his slow-maturing talent, was perhaps
without an equal in this country. He was at his best on the least formal
of occasions in the Sunday evening sermons in the church at Buckfast.
The impeded character of his English speech was in itself an asset. He
could not be fluent, and the congregation would hang upon his words
as he sought, and always successfully, for the phrase which might carry
the meaning of his rich and charming thought. He had an approach
which was profoundly theological and confidence-inspiring. The level
of his utterance was remarkable and reflected with an almost rugged
calm his hard-wrought and unfacile processes. High as is the compliment, there was something nearly Pauline in Abbot Anscar as his words
ground forward. No other preacher has given me the impression of the
grinding of the mills of God.

'He had a serene prudence and a charity which was determined and
unquenchable. His character reflected those specifically Teutonic
virtues to which the Catholic Church has owed so much. But in thinking of him the mind returns to the German richness of his thought.
The Catholic tradition was his heritage; and he meditated on, and gave
to us, the word of God.'

CHAPTER XII

THE MONK AND THE ABBOT

NOT many books of purely human inspiration have made an impact upon the history of Europe such as that made by the Rule of St Benedict, if indeed it is really accurate to describe that wonderful volume as a work of purely human inspiration. Apart from the divinely inspired books of the Old and the New Testament, no book has so profoundly affected the lives of so many people as the precious volume drawn up by Benedict of Norcia on the lofty heights of Monte Cassino more than fourteen centuries ago. Favoured though he was with prophetic powers, it is unlikely that the Saint had any idea of the magnitude of his achievement when he founded what he modestly describes as 'a school of the service of God'—*dominici schola servitii*. From that remote day down to our own, countless men and women—the latter even in greater numbers—have flocked to this admirable school and graduated, within its sheltering walls, in the highest science of all—the science of the Saints.

Nor is St Benedict's school an exclusive institution; on the contrary, it is open to all men of good will since only one condition is required for admission—though it is an indispensable one: the aspirant must be one who truly seeks God—*si revera Deum quaerit* (*Regula*, LVIII). In this pregnant sentence the Patriarch of monks condenses the whole philosophy of the religious life. The monk who forgoes the companionship of men does so under pressure of an urge not unlike that which drives men to explore the unknown regions of the earth or to climb mountain peaks inaccessible to ordinary mortals. The monk is out on the most thrilling of quests—the quest for God: *si revera Deum quaerit*.

It could not be expected that when young Martin Vonier left home and country for the cloister he was explicitly actuated by considerations such as those just described, but he undoubtedly knew that life in a monastery implies a striving after a higher and stricter standard of piety and virtue than that which is required from all Christians. His sister testified that from his early years he showed an earnestness and a gravity above his age. On the other hand, he himself was always extraordinarily chary of information about his own person. He has left no diary or record of any kind which would throw light upon his spiritual development, and with the sole exception of his letters to the Abbess of Dourgne and to his sister, a nun of the Convent of the Assumption in Paris, no letters of his have been preserved to help the biographer in an attempt to draw a reasonably live portrait of the man, so that he must perforce draw upon personal recollections and impressions. These, as a matter of fact, cover the whole of the Abbot's life at Buckfast, beginning in October 1891, when we were both in the alumnate of the Abbey.

It was not easy to pierce through the reserve and reticence with which Dom Anscar seemed bent on protecting his intimate self, hence anything approaching real intimacy was well-nigh impossible. But it was not always so. There was a period, though not of long duration, when he was far more communicative than in the latter part of his life. During that first period his rôle in a conversation would not be exclusively that of a good listener. 'I have always disliked chatter' (meaning mere talk), he once wrote to the Abbess of Dourgne; but if the subject of the conversation was a worth-while one, or if he meant to unbend, or to contribute to the talk at recreation, he could take his full share in it. Shortly after his profession he was appointed assistant to the novice-master, who was also the Superior of the house. For some time the present writer was the only novice. I have always cherished grateful recollections of the many lengthy conversations I then had with him on religious, devotional and theological subjects, so much so indeed that I sometimes feel that it was at this time that I learnt all the theology I know.

At this period, that is, at about the turn of the century, life at Buckfast was exceedingly austere. Silence as strict as that of a Trappist monastery was enforced at all times and in all places. There was no formal recreation, and only on a few days in the course of the year were the novices and the young professed monks granted an afternoon's walk, when one could talk freely, but the drawback was that one was made to make a kind of forced march with never a break: you simply were in motion all the time and to suggest a halt for a brief rest would have been regarded as a weakness incompatible with monastic strength of character. There was indeed a period of so-called 'free time', after the midday meal, when we walked solemnly and silently up and down a garden path, first saying the rosary, after which we might read an improving book. Everyone, too, seemed to stake out his own pitch, hence one could read a book without risking to stumble against a tree or another silent walker. I well remember Dom Anscar telling me—in a bout of confidence—that with a view to cutting out all distracting or idle thoughts, he would from that day onwards read none but spiritual books. One of these books was St Augustine's 'Confessions'—in Latin, of course. Such a recreation could not 're-create', though it had the advantage, the only one I now think, that it enabled one to read books which otherwise one would not have had time to peruse. On the other hand, it was probably this practice that was at least a contributory cause—if it was not the main one—of those distressing headaches which, already at this period, used to incapacitate Dom Anscar for a couple of days at a time and from which he was never completely cured.

A monk is a seeker after God. To this quest Dom Anscar applied himself from the first day of his monastic life. Without a trace of affectation, with utter absence of what might be construed as rigorism, not to say fanaticism, he carried out the duties of each recurring day with an exactness and a regularity that did not really strike the beholder precisely because it was an everyday spectacle. I cannot recollect a single instance of a Superior having had occasion to take him to task for any breach of the Rule or of the established routine of the house. This does not mean that he did not pay toll to human frailty by involuntary mistakes, or that he never got on other people's nerves by some oddity. The only thing for which I know him to have been rebuked on occasion was his lack of what is called 'custody of the eyes': he once told me, as Abbot, that custody of the eyes was 'a French virtue'! I think what he meant was that our French Superiors were for ever insisting, in exaggerated terms, on the evil of using one's eyes to see what was going on around one. As a matter of fact, he certainly never acquired that virtue, so much so that people occasionally commented on the fact that the Abbot was always looking about, even when carrying out a pontifical function. In this respect he was certainly unlike the ecclesiastics and prelates of whom the biographers are wont to say that they were apparently unaware of their surroundings and never raised an eye as they moved about the sanctuary. On the other hand, I am certain that Abbot Vonier's mental concentration was such that it was in no way hindered or interrupted by the sight of people and things.

To be able to sing, or to be tone-deaf, is not a matter of indifference

for a Benedictine monk since the solemn celebration of the Liturgy—
'the Work of God'—*Opus Dei* as St Benedict calls it—occupies so
many hours of his day and indeed constitutes the most important
occupation of his whole life. An ear for music and a good singing voice
are therefore valuable assets, though not indispensable ones, for a man
may make up for this deficiency by some other qualities. The predecessor of the present Abbot Primate of our Order never succeeded
in singing the *Preface*, or the *Pater noster* of the Mass in anything even
remotely like the official tune. Dom Anscar's aptitude for the chant
was strictly limited—but his keenness made up, to some extent, for
natural skill. Largely owing to the smallness of members in the community, he occasionally officiated as cantor. In this sphere his zeal far
exceeded his aptitude. While still in the alumnate, and as a novice, he
was one of the regular organists, though he confined his operations to
the harmonium and, as far as memory serves, never 'presided' at the
organ. He applied himself to this activity with his wonted earnestness,
but his efforts were not rewarded by any marked success. He was too
intelligent not to be aware of his limitations, and I believe he shared
the brethren's sense of relief when he was informed that his services
were no longer required. It was he, however, who conducted the
novices' singing classes. His knowledge of the theory of plain chant
was considerable, but the practical execution of it left much to be
desired.

In view of his early training and of the prevailing ethos at that period
of the history of Buckfast, it was inevitable that his views of monastic
life should have been rather narrow and unduly rigid. It was with something akin to a shock that one heard him observe, more than once, that
if St Benedict were to return to earth, he would not feel at home with
those who glory in his name and call themselves his children, but
rather with the Trappists, who, he asserted, alone fully measure up to
the standards of life set up by the Patriarch of monks. Such an attitude
is understandable if we remember that up to the time of his ordination
and his subsequent Roman experience, he had had no contact whatsoever with other Benedictines, whilst some of the older monks of Buckfast—all of them Frenchmen—had somehow managed to create an
impression in the minds of the younger generation that outside the
French Province of the Cassinese Congregation Benedictine life fell
far short of the ideal set before us by St Benedict.

At this time, that is, between 1882 and 1900, the small community of
Buckfast had no independent existence but was regarded as an integral

part of the parent community of La Pierre-qui-Vire, whose Abbot was therefore the canonical Superior of Buckfast. This prelate resided in France and his visits and sojourns at Buckfast were of rare occurrence and short duration. One consequence of this unsatisfactory situation was that a monk could fairly easily pass from one house to the other, or be transferred by superiors. So there came a time when it became known that if anyone would volunteer to help in the revival of the parent community in France, his offer would be welcome. Only one young priest actually volunteered, but for a while Dom Anscar also seems to have toyed with the idea. I have a vivid recollection of a conversation with him on the subject. One shudders retrospectively at the thought of what such a step would have meant for Buckfast, but Providence, which had marked him off for a great task, prevented him from taking a decision which, humanly speaking, would have had disastrous consequences for this monastery.

The thought of offering himself to the Abbot of La Pierre-qui-Vire was little more than a passing mood arising from a mental picture of a house situate in the midst of a vast solitude, where he would have been able to apply himself without let or hindrance to the two things he valued most—prayer and study. On the other hand he also realized the truth of St Benedict's weighty saying, to the effect that God can be served equally well in any place—*in omni loco uni Domino servitur, uni Regi militatur* (*Reg.* LXI). It was no momentary feeling, but a profound conviction that caused him, many years later, to write to the Abbess of Dourgne in these terms: 'I hold that, in principle, any soul may realize its vocation in the Benedictine life—provided it finds the true Benedictine life.' In another letter to the same correspondent he goes so far as to write: 'In my opinion you [that is the community of St Scholastica's of Dourgne] realize the whole of the Catholic ideal, more than . . .' and he mentions an Order the name of which had better be omitted since comparisons are odious, but it is one for which he cherished a deep affection and sincere admiration.

Letters to his sister written during his stay in Rome bear witness to his profound appreciation of the monastic life. On the termination of his studies at Sant' Anselmo his Superiors ordered him to pay a visit to his aged parents in Germany. It required a formal command, for he had made a vow never to visit his home and country. From their common home he wrote to his sister in Paris: 'Here I am, *en route* for England and my own monastic home. God be praised! I cannot tell you how greatly I yearn to take up once more the peaceful, sanctifying life of the cloister. . . . My dear Sister, do join me in thanking God for the signal grace He is about to bestow upon me within the next few days—namely the grace of returning to my own monastery. You are blessed in that you never need leave your convent—it is a further reason for you to be at all times most faithful in corresponding with the grace of the Holy Spirit and always to pray much for me.'

Another letter, also written from Rome a few months earlier, during the jubilee year of 1900, at the beginning of which Leo XIII had consecrated the whole of mankind to the Sacred Heart of Jesus, is of particular interest because it gives us a clue to his ideals and aspirations in this, the third year of his priesthood. His greatly loved sister was a humble lay sister who was wont to spend long working hours in the kitchen of a big convent, complete with school and lady-boarders—the latter including a temperamental Spanish princess. 'Since you are so happy in your lowly estate,' he wrote, 'you can help me greatly by your prayers in order that, with God's help, I may be able to do something, nay much, for the honour of His Name and to win souls for Him. Alas! how barren, up to now, my life as a priest appears to me. You know well that you can give me no greater satisfaction than that which I experience when I am assured that you are drawing ever closer to God. I fail to understand how it is possible to love a person that is not quickened and adorned by the grace of God.' The latter sentiment may surprise the reader, but I have heard him speak in the same strain on more than one occasion. He then proceeds: 'In July I shall be passing through Paris, when I return to the bosom of my beloved monastic family. You have my permission to importunate Our Lord with requests that He may allow us to meet, be it for never so short a time, only do not importunate me! If God in His goodness grants us this satisfaction, I shall be able to talk to you at leisure about all the beautiful and holy things one sees in Rome. In the meantime I shall go on praying for you and your Sisters [viz. the Nuns of the Assumption] at the tombs of the Holy Apostles, Martyrs and Virgins. It is such a happiness to be so close to these great friends of Our Lord.

'I have already seen the Holy Father on two occasions, and at close quarters. But you must understand that the Pope could do nothing for the salvation of the world if there were no holy souls hidden away in their convents, who never cease to plead for mercy and who can achieve wonderful things even while at work in a kitchen.'

In these opening years of his life as a priest he seems to have been drawn in two apparently opposite directions, namely, towards a strictly monastic and contemplative life on the one hand, and on the other to active apostolic work. On 7th January 1903, a belated Christmas and New Year's letter opens on a sombre note: 'What will the year that has just begun bring forth both for you and for your Sisters?' he asks. This was the era of the persecution and expulsion of religious communities of men and women, to which Auteuil, Sister Swithbert's convent, with many others, was to fall a victim. He then goes on: 'But however badly things may go in the world here below, God's blissfulness is not diminished in any way, and He will always raise up souls upon which He will pour out the gifts which so many foolish people reject. If His friends are few in number, may they prove good, and very good friends of His. The thought is St Teresa's and it is your brother's New Year's gift to you. And since I mention St Teresa, I would have you join me in worrying that good Saint,[1] whom I have been importuning for some time on behalf of several souls dear to me. Up to now she has turned a deaf ear to my entreaties. Therefore, as soon as you get this letter, you will ask leave from whomsoever it may concern, to make a novena for all the Carmelite nuns that may be in Purgatory, so as to move their Mother, St Teresa. I invariably proceed after this fashion. . . . Now I don't want to hear from you unless you are able to assure me that you have begun the novena and that you go on with it with grim determination.' He then tells her of Dom Boniface Natter's election as first Abbot of the new Buckfast. 'This election,' he writes, 'makes me leap for joy . . . however, there is another promotion which I mention with less enthusiasm. Four months ago I was given the office of procurator. In that capacity I have to make debts and pay them, sell and buy cows, busy myself with the kitchen, go to the bank, make bargains, and heaven knows what not. You will laugh at me, but you had better pity me and pray for me. However, obedience means life everlasting; but I would rather apply my mind to other things than these futilities.'

In the early autumn of 1904 Abbot Boniface was instructed to accompany the Abbot General of our Congregation on a visitation of one of our monasteries in the United States. His absence of about three months threw yet more mundane occupations upon one whose tastes carried him in a very different direction. On 22nd September he informed his sister of the additional responsibilities thrust upon him. At this time Sister Swithbert was herself undergoing a severe trial the exact nature

[1] 'Je voudrais que vous vous unissiez à moi pour casser la tête à cette bonne sainte.' I know of no English equivalent to this vigorous French expression.

of which is not specified in the letter but which seems to have been of a spiritual kind. In her distress she had evidently sought help from her priest-brother. 'Alas! my dear Sister,' he wrote, 'I am particularly unfitted to comfort you, for I dread suffering—especially the kind of suffering you have to endure just now. However, I retain sufficient good sense to realize that in a similar situation the wisest thing would be to believe that Our Lord is resolved to mould our souls in His own image. With this end in view He makes use of means whose efficacy He alone knows, while we experience their searching action which, in point of fact, lasts only for a time. The sun is sure to return, more radiant than ever precisely because the soul's atmosphere will have been purified. Moreover, if we undertake to save and sanctify souls at any cost we assume a grievous burden. But think of the happiness of even one single soul saved through the perfection of yours, when that soul comes to be admitted to the everlasting vision of God and thereupon realizes that it owes its happiness to you. This shows you how great my gratitude to you will be one day.'

It was also in a letter from Rome, a few days before Christmas 1905, hence only a few months before the catastrophe that was to affect the course of his life so profoundly, that he speaks of another apostolic activity than that of prayer. He was teaching philosophy, hence his occupations were all of the intellectual order. 'The only tools I handle,' he wrote, 'are books, except, of course, the implements of the refectory. If this kind of thing lasts I shall start writing books which you may then read for your instruction, provided you have the necessary patience.' The idea of taking up his pen was taking definite shape in his mind. He cherished a strong love for Rome, the spiritual capital of the world and the hub of the Church's life and activity, hence he was quite willing to spend at least a few years in teaching philosophy to the interesting young men whom their Superiors were sending to the Eternal City in the hope that, on their return to their respective monasteries, they would be the means of maintaining a high standard of intellectual life in their communities. He was well aware that his abbot would do his utmost to secure his return to Buckfast at the earliest opportunity, but for the time being he welcomed the temporary release from the material occupations which were so little to his liking. However, before many months were over, the tragedy of the *Sirio* was to put an abrupt end to his teaching activities in Rome and to open up for him a far wider field of action.

When in September 1906 Dom Anscar was chosen to succeed Abbot

Boniface Natter, he was not quite thirty-one years of age, so that he was the youngest abbot in the whole Benedictine Order. Thus also his life as an ordinary monk comprised a mere dozen years and he had been a priest for only eight years. It is no disparagement of even so outstanding a personality as Abbot Vonier's if one ventures to think that it would have been a great advantage, both for himself and the community he was destined to rule, if he had had a more protracted experience of the life of an ordinary religious—that is, the life of one who holds no office in the house but just leads the quiet, uneventful, perhaps one might say monotonous, existence which in the very nature of things is that of the majority of the members of a religious house. One would think that experience of this kind is indispensable for one called to exercise absolute authority for the rest of his days. It must be obvious to anyone who gives the matter serious thought that the seemingly peaceful and sheltered life of a religious is not without its own peculiar difficulties, and that it is therefore expedient that the Superior should know them from personal experience, for in this way he can best learn the art of blending wisdom and prudence with strength and gentleness, which are the constituent elements of that discretion which St Benedict calls the mother of virtues. On the other hand, the task for which divine Providence had so manifestly destined—and almost miraculously preserved—the subject of this book, was one of such magnitude as to need not only all the natural buoyancy, not to say venturesomeness and impetuosity of youth, to initiate it, but likewise the prospect of long years, if it was to be carried to a successful issue. Happily in the present instance there was no risk in the choice of one so young for so high and arduous an office, for wisdom is not necessarily or exclusively the appanage of old age: 'Venerable old age,' says the Wise Man in the Bible, 'is not that of long time, nor counted by the number of years, but the understanding of a man is grey hairs' (Wisd. iv. 8–9).

St Benedict defines the rôle of the abbot of a monastery in a pregnant sentence: 'The abbot,' he says, 'is believed to hold the place of Christ in the monastery'—*Christi agere vices in monasterio creditur* (*Reg.* II). In the present context *creditur* does not mean a pious belief or opinion, but a firm conviction. Incidentally this definition gives us the measure of the value—of the worth-whileness so to speak—of the religious life, for if the abbot impersonates Christ Himself and acts in His place, it needs must follow that as long as he is faithful to his Rule and lives under obedience to his Superior, every conscious action of a monk is performed in the direct service of Christ and is thus an act of worship of 'the true King' whose paladin the monk becomes on the day on which he dons what St Benedict describes as 'the shining armour of obedience'—*Christo vero Regi militaturus . . . obedientiae fortissima atque praeclara arma . . . (Reg. Prologus)*. With this definition of the abbatial office and of the monk's duty, St Benedict lays down the fundamental principle of monastic government, and all he has to say in Chapters II and LXIV is but a development of this constitutional basis. In a Benedictine house, therefore, the abbot's rôle is of paramount importance precisely because in the Benedictine Order every community forms a unit apart and constitutes a real *familia* of which the abbot—as his name implies—is the father. Thus it comes about that the strength and vitality, the tone and tendency of a Benedictine monastery, depend on the character of its abbot to an extent that cannot but be a source of anxious thought for the man on whose shoulders so grievous a responsibility is laid. A scholarly Benedictine abbot of our own time—one deeply versed in monastic history—does not hesitate to affirm that 'history proclaims emphatically and eloquently that (by the test of a working success) St Benedict has been amply justified in all the ages . . . it becomes clear that the great majority of abbots must have realized in some measure St Benedict's hopes, because the great sweep of Benedictine history could not by any possibility have been what it has been had the system been vitiated at the core. The abbot is the very heart of St Benedict's institute; and no institution could have thriven and worked and flourished during fourteen centuries and had such a history as the Benedictines have, if all along it was labouring under chronic heart disease' (Abbot C. Butler, *Benedictine Monachism*, p. 194).

This somewhat lengthy digression is not beside the point because it gives the reader some idea of the responsibilities the youthful Abbot of Buckfast assumed on the day of his election by his brethren, nor was the elect himself unaware of the weight of the burden. However, when asked by the president of the Chapter whether he was willing to assent to the choice made of him, Dom Anscar replied that though he would be far happier if he were to continue as he was, an ordinary monk, he felt that it was God's will that he should accept the office.

The election needed confirmation by the Abbot General, so whilst awaiting that final sanction Dom Anscar stayed first at Ilfracombe and later, for a few days, at St Scholastica's Abbey, Teignmouth. On his return, in the afternoon of 17th October, he was given a great welcome by the community and the villagers. On this occasion he told the community that he could assure them, in St Paul's words, that he came 'not to exercise dominion over your faith, but to be a helper of your joy' (2 Cor. i. 23). On the following day, after he had been canonically installed as Abbot of Buckfast, he declared that it was his firm conviction that through charity and unity among ourselves we would be able to face with the utmost confidence whatever the future might have in store for us as a community. The words sound as if the speaker had been momentarily moved by a breath of the spirit of prophecy.

Not many days after his installation the new abbot took steps to enhance the solemnity of the daily liturgy. Up till then the daily Conventual Mass had been a Low Mass. From All Saints' Day this Mass was to be a *Missa Cantata*. Vespers also were to be sung daily, and before long the day concluded with sung Compline. This has been our practice ever since, and a few years after the opening of the new church the *Missa Cantata* became a full High Mass. These measures, so eminently in keeping with the Benedictine spirit and monastic tradition, were but the outward expression of his own vivid sense of man's duty to his Creator and of what the Church has a right to expect from a religious body such as a Benedictine community. Several years later, in a Christmas letter to the Abbess of Dourgne, he lamented the fact that 'there are so few people who understand that the soul's highest activity is to glorify Our Lord. *You* have had the grace to understand this, and your daughters are worthy of you. One might almost think that in these days people are so preoccupied with God's interests—as if they were in a bad way—that they forget the duty of glorifying Him. Yet we should understand that we can never be more than God's tools in the realization of His designs and that the only thing that is perfectly clear is our duty to glorify Him.'

In December 1934, one month after his sixtieth birthday, he wrote to the same correspondent: 'Sixty years! what an awful thought: Yet I am in better health than when I was only thirty. If things go on like this I shall be able to do yet a great deal of work in Holy Church. . . .' He could not know that he would see only four more birthdays, but the letter reveals in unmistakable terms the nature of the programme he had set himself when he took up the government of his Abbey. The overriding ambition of his life was none other than to promote the glory of God by every means in his power. His building activities sprang from no other motive.

It was in the nature of things that these activities should catch the eye and win for him the admiration of the outside world, but they were by no means the ones that held the first place in his mind, for he was profoundly conscious of his duty to his community. Whatever an abbot's interests may be, his first and essential duty is to be a father to his religious family since he is appointed not so much in order to exercise authority over it as to promote the high purpose for which its members are banded together: *sciat sibi oportere prodesse magis quam praeesse*, says St Benedict (*Reg.* LXIV).

During most of the thirty-two years of his rule Abbot Vonier was never without temporal solicitudes—I would not call them 'anxieties', for, as he observed more than once, he never worried but relied on God with childlike confidence. As a matter of fact it was one of the most remarkable traits of his character that he never—perhaps I should say hardly ever—complained either of people or events. But though he did not complain or defend himself—at least not publicly—he was by no means insensitive to criticism when echoes of it came to his ears. As early as Christmas 1913 he wrote to Dourgne: 'People reproach me with not being practical: little do they know me. I grant that details of administration are a trial to me, but I can understand the practical needs of a Benedictine community as well as anybody. However, what does it matter what people think? It is possible to carry out successfully a very great and useful piece of work while under the shadow of a cloud.' This is true enough: moreover, one runs no risk of sunstroke while working under the shadow of a cloud, but if the cloud is compounded of suspicion and disapproval in high places, its shadow might well have depressed a less buoyant and magnanimous nature.

Abbot Anscar felt it his duty to temper the excessive rigour of the life of his community, so as to suit and proportion its demands to the strength of the present generation. In this matter he did not act lightly or impetuously; on the contrary, before taking a decisive step he sought advice, even medical advice; but when he had come to the conclusion that he must act, he did not hesitate to do so, though he knew well that he would meet with strong and persistent opposition both from within and without. In one of his letters to Dourgne he speaks of the intransigence of good people whose minds are so petrified that they are incapable of assimilating a new idea, or adapting themselves to a new situation. This is the cloud referred to in the letter quoted above. In the end, when 'the great and useful work' had been brought to a successful issue, the cloud lifted and his last years were brightened by the approval even of those who, at one time, had misunderstood his character and misjudged his intentions.

The Abbot was as happy in his rôle as a builder as in that of a writer and a preacher, for in every one of these capacities he was a creator and his ultimate purpose, though pursued in different mediums, was identical. On 19th January 1930 he wrote to Dourgne: 'Your dear letter had on me an effect not unlike that of strong gusts of wind such as we have been experiencing of late in this part of the country. You say that mine is the soul of a founder! No one has ever told me such a thing, nor has it ever occurred to my own mind—but it makes me think hard. As a matter of fact, I have now been Abbot for the space of twenty-four years. I greatly fear that I shall leave a permanent impression on Buckfast—all the more so as when I came on the scene it was little more than a shapeless mass, for none of my predecessors has had time to do anything.' 'The soul of a founder'! The compliment was the Lady Abbess's thanks for a tribute he had paid her two years earlier when, after a flying visit to Dourgne, he had told her that hers was the immense privilege of being able to create something from the beginning. 'How one wearies of the business of mending and repairing,' he wrote; 'that business has been inflicted on us all through the last three weeks.[1] At last, in a couple of hours, we shall be free, all of us, to return to real life.' A little later he assured the Abbess that her convent was the most beautiful thing he had seen in the course of his extensive travels that year, and in his Christmas letter he declared that his visit to Dourgne had been *the* event of the year 1928. 'All the rest,' he declared, 'held but little interest for me.'

What he thought of his work as a 'founder' or 'a creator' may be gathered from a letter written at the time of his abbatial silver jubilee: 'I have been able to carry out successfully almost everything I wanted to do for this community [of Buckfast] in the course of these twenty-five years. But I share your conviction that it is to Dom Boniface's sacrifice that my success is ultimately to be ascribed.' The letter ends with a request for prayers. 'I beg your prayers, so that the second part of my abbacy may make up for the deficiencies of the first.' He was well aware that even God's work normally requires time. As a matter of fact, history is there to show that many, if not most of the men and women who have done great things have also been granted length of years—St Benedict might head the long list that could be drawn up. It was only natural that Abbot Anscar should wish to complete what

[1] The letter was written on the last day of a lengthy General Chapter.

he had initiated in the face of so many difficulties. He had been abbot for not quite four years when he wrote: 'When I compare myself now with what I was less than four years ago, what a change I perceive! But all my personal vicissitudes have only served to strengthen my attachment to your person and to your community. For the rest, I am a cold and calculating individual. I am amazed at the affection shown to me on all sides. On the other hand I think that both here [viz. at Buckfast] and elsewhere there are those who do not trust me and my ideas. However, up to now I have been invariably successful in everything I have put my hand to. I understand that it has been said here that the man who succeeds me will have a difficult task. I myself have always felt that God, in His goodness, will give me all the time I need for carrying all I have undertaken to a successful termination. Not the least of these undertakings is to put the observance on a satisfactory footing, so that the Rule will not be an obstacle to vocations but a means to the salvation of souls. Why should not we have the beautiful monastic life of the "garden enclosed"? [1] Your wisdom has been visibly blessed by God. . . . Is there anything more beautiful than the Benedictine life? We do not need anything else.' And he concludes: 'Pray for me always. I do not know whether Our Lord is pleased with me, but He will forgive everything for the love He bears a chosen soul.'

This letter is one of the very few in which he really lets his heart speak; only his deep affection and admiration for a truly great Abbess and an admirable community of nuns could have caused him to break through that calculated, shy reserve which he observed when speaking of himself or of his deeper emotions. A letter written a few days before 8th September is equally revealing: 'It gives me great joy to send you my good wishes for the feast of the Nativity of the Mother of God because in the birth of the Blessed Virgin I see mysteries of grace and love which make me think instinctively of the virgin souls which Our Lord has chosen for Himself from the moment of their baptism. So you will be very much in my mind when the choir sings *Nativitas est hodie sanctae Mariae Virginis*. Your beautiful religious life is a faithful reproduction of that of the glorious Virgin—it is a ray of light and comfort in the midst of the world's darkness.'

The Abbey church was the Abbot's chief preoccupation from the first day of his rule, but it did not cause him to overlook the need of more living-space for a rapidly increasing community. He accordingly

---

[1] *Hortus conclusus*: the reference is to Canticle iv. 12. It was his favourite description of St Scholastica's Abbey, Dourgne, and it gave the Abbess immense pleasure.

erected, in two stages, the east wing of the monastery upon the ancient foundations which for three and a half centuries had lain hid several feet beneath the soil and had thus been preserved for the day when they would bear the weight of the restored Abbey.[1] To the south of the Abbey he also put up a structure of considerable size though not of any marked architectural beauty. This building houses various industries. There are rooms where the produce of a large apiary is extracted, stored, bottled and despatched; rooms where the tonic wine is made; the clothes-room, a bookbinder's shop, the Brothers' recreation-room, a weaving-shed where silk for liturgical vestments is woven, and lastly, rooms where pianists can exercise their skill without disturbing anyone. The supreme advantage of this building is that it masks to some extent the sight, and even somewhat deadens the noise of the machinery, of the nearby factory.

A letter written in 1926 to a would-be aspirant, an army chaplain then stationed at Cairo, shows that he was revolving plans for an even weightier enterprise. Through the munificence of the late Henry Schiller, who had already done so much for the Abbey church, the community had recently come into possession of about two hundred acres of farmland on the left bank of the River Dart, which up till then had marked the boundary of the Abbey property. The Abbot's correspondent, whose letter has not been preserved, had had some experience as a schoolmaster and had evidently suggested that Buckfast should follow the example of other Benedictine abbeys by opening a school. In his letter the Abbot said: 'Yes, we are full of the thought that the land we are acquiring may become the site of a big school in time to come. We form mental pictures without end of that future.' However, as far as can be ascertained, he never spoke of these plans to the community, though he may have done so in the course of private conversation. Be this as it may, he concludes: 'I feel that for several years to come my work for the Abbey will continue to be of a preparatory and pioneering character and, shall I say it? I do not feel quite ready for you. I should like you to serve your full term as a

---

[1] Justice and gratitude alike demand that it should be put on record that this work was only made possible through the admirable generosity of two ladies, the Misses Strickland, who sold their house and gave the price to the Abbot, to enable him to begin the construction of the east wing of the Abbey. The two sisters then went to live, and eventually ended their holy lives, in a small wood-and-corrugated-iron bungalow. These two saintly women cherished a wonderful devotion to St Joseph. As a result of the First World War they lost all their income, which came to them from investments in Jamaica—but they were not dismayed: 'St Joseph would not forget them'—nor was their trust misplaced. The Abbot likewise received immense assistance from another princely benefactress whose name I dare not set down here since she is still happily with us.

chaplain, the end of which should coincide with the maturing of much of our work here.'

Six more years were to elapse before the completion of the church. By that time the Abbot was a very sick man, and though mentally as alert and as vigorous as ever, his physical decline was very pronounced. What is certain is that he never took any steps, even remote ones, towards the realization of an undertaking of such magnitude as the opening of a school.

Manifold and absorbing as were the Abbot's occupations in the material sphere, they did not by any means cause him to neglect the duties for which he was primarily appointed—that is the spiritual and material care of a family of which he was the father. As we have seen above, the abbot, in St Benedict's words, plays the part of Christ in the monastery. Now one of the main concerns of Our Lord, during the years of His public life, was the training and formation of His immediate followers—the Apostles. Such also is an abbot's chief task, hence St Benedict insists that he must be 'learned in the Law of God'— *oportet eum esse doctum in lege divina*, 'so that he may know whence to bring forth new things and old'. This basic quality Abbot Anscar possessed in full measure. The Bible had been his favourite reading from his youth, and for many years he read it in the original text— Greek and Hebrew—but in later years he made a point of reading it in English so as to be able to quote with ease the official translation. His familiarity with the *Summa* of St Thomas was amazing; moreover, to all his reading he brought not only a keen intelligence but likewise an uncommonly retentive memory—a faculty without which there can be no real erudition since, as Dante has it, 'to understand but not to retain is not knowledge'. Thus, in spite of his youth, Dom Anscar was well equipped for the rôle of a teacher and guide of souls. This duty he discharged most faithfully up to the last weeks of his life. At the very beginning of his rule he undertook to give the weekly—or almost weekly—theological conference prescribed by Canon Law. In this way he lectured on practically the whole of the *Summa* of St Thomas. For years also, morning after morning, he expounded the short passage of the Rule of St Benedict which is read at the end of Prime—that is, up to 1933, when we ceased to go to Chapter for the second part of that office. His was no mere literary or historical explanation of that admirable little book; on the contrary, he managed to give the community what practically amounted to a systematic course of ascetical teaching based on and inspired by the masterpiece in which the Patriarch of Western monachism concentrated all the wisdom and experience of his own long life as well as the experience of previous centuries. It is greatly to be regretted that no written record of these conferences has been preserved, but he always spoke extempore, while the time and place did not favour deep mental concentration on the part of the listeners and completely ruled out all possibility of taking notes there and then.

What was the general character of these intimate allocutions and exhortations? The answer is that they were in line with his published writings. There was nothing petty or narrow in his teaching. He never advocated any of the many 'devotions' which flower so profusely in the Church's garden. Not that he scorned these holy practices—far from it. He never missed his rosary and visited the Blessed Sacrament daily; for many years he also made the Stations of the Cross every day. His was a truly 'Catholic' spirit, in the devotional sphere no less than in the intellectual. Just as he belonged to no 'school' of theology, so did he not follow any particular 'school' of spirituality or prayer, for unfortunately there are 'schools' in this sphere. His spirituality was that of the gospel—whole, pure, undiluted—and, when one comes to think of it, do we need any other manual of spirituality? For some people this is much too simple: they want to establish a system, lay down an order of procedure, put up signposts to the right and to the left in a region in which the Holy Spirit prompts and inspires, rules and reigns alone. Advice and guidance the Abbot would give when consulted, but he was ever respectful of that fundamental freedom of the human soul of which St Paul speaks: 'Where the Lord's Spirit is, there is freedom' (2 Cor. iii. 17); in a word, if I may so put it, he did not believe in keeping souls, as it were, on leading-strings.

This would be the place to speak of the Abbot's own spiritual life; but here the biographer encounters his greatest difficulty, for if, as we have seen, Dom Anscar was at all times extremely reticent about his own person, he was even more reserved about matters that concerned no one except himself and God. Unlike some other notable personages of our time, he has left no written record which would give us a picture of his interior life, hence the only key to his soul's attitude to, and his relations with, Almighty God are his sermons and retreat conferences and, of course, his published works. It may seem to be going too far, yet I cannot help thinking that, with suitable adaptations and qualifications, one might apply to the subject of this book the encomium with which St Gregory the Great concludes his all too brief biography of

St Benedict: 'This I want you to know,' the great Pope writes, 'that not the least of his achievements was the wisdom of his teaching . . . hence if anyone wishes to become more intimately acquainted with his manner of life, he may find all the information he wishes for in his Rule, for the teaching of so sincere and forthright a man could not but be a picture and an outward revelation of his inner life.' [1]

The only really intimate documents on which any kind of assessment of his spiritual life could be based are the letters to his sister and to the Abbess of Dourgne, but even his longest letters are little more than brief notes, often written in haste. But these precious literary remains suggest a mental picture of a man whose whole attitude to life was based on a lively sense of the reality and nearness of the supernatural order. I do not hesitate to affirm that, by and large, his whole life was that of one who, like the patriarch spoken of in the Book of Genesis, 'walked with God', and that this fact is the true explanation of his taciturnity, gravity and reserve. He would not, or rather could not, 'let himself go', so to speak, or throw himself into anything with the whole of himself because the thought of God was habitually at the back of his mind. He was undoubtedly one of the most unworldly persons one could hope to meet. He had a positive horror of whatever savoured of worldliness; in fact, in this respect he sometimes saw or suspected worldliness where a sense of humour—and he was not without such a sense—would have spared him unnecessary alarm.

It is a characteristic of a magnanimous soul that it can suffer in silence. Abbot Vonier possessed this admirable quality in a high degree. It is no small tribute to a man if it can be said of him that he never complained either of persons, or things and circumstances, and that he was gloriously immune from the weakling's habit of self-pity. Abbot Vonier was so self-contained, or self-sufficient, that one might have thought he was insensible to the buffets of adversity or to the pinpricks of criticism. However, his admirable equanimity was not due to insensibility, still less to an attitude of lofty contempt for what people might say or do: his Olympian calm and serenity sprang from just plain Christian fortitude. He once told me that if he never lost his temper, the reason was that he could not afford to do so—it would give him a bad headache! In the whole of his correspondence with the Abbess of Dourgne there is only one instance when he refers to his

[1] *Cujus si quis velit subtilius mores vitamque cognoscere, potest in eadem institutione Regulae omnes magisterii illius actus invenire, quia sanctus vir nullomodo potuit aliter docere quam vixit* (Dial. II, 36).

trials, but if he mentions them at all, the context makes it clear that he does not do so because he wishes to be condoled with: 'In the course of this year,' he writes at the end of 1912, 'I have suffered more than during the whole of the preceding thirty-four [sic] years of my life. So I have learnt a lesson; and the chief thing I learnt is that a man can ambition no greater privilege than that of being Our Lord's instrument in the execution of His mysterious designs.' And he adds: 'I shall become a contemplative once more—but on a much broader basis than formerly. No existence would please me more than a purely intellectual life—but to be kept down to earth by temporal worries . . .' The sentence is left unfinished. In another letter, written exactly five years before his death, he says: 'I should like to be young again and to take up the life of a young monk!' As a matter of fact he once told one of the older Fathers: 'I am a contemplative,' but, he added, 'this is a secret of the King'—adapting a text in Tob. xii. 7. 'If one wants to become a saint,' he wrote to the Abbess of Dourgne, 'one should welcome public humiliations. One should not be spoilt by everybody, or be the object of so much affection. May Our Lord prompt you to remind me of all the things in which He knows me to be deficient!'

If he really desired public humiliations or at least felt the need or usefulness of them, it may be said that they were not altogether spared him. Over a period of several years both he, and the community with him, were the objects of a malevolent campaign of calumny of a particularly odious character, so much so in fact that, after suffering in silence, he was at length prevailed upon to invoke the protection of the law. On this occasion he gave proof of a magnanimity which many of his friends found excessive. But he was incapable of vindictiveness and so was content with the public vindication of his own and the community's honour, preferring to leave retribution to God. On the other hand he was fully conscious of the magnitude of his achievement as a builder and of his extraordinary success in the literary sphere. Yet in 1910 he could write: 'I have now been Abbot for a term of four years. Much has been accomplished in that time, but everything seems to have been done not by my hand but by that of another—the hand of an unseen abbot whose grave is the Mediterranean.' He then makes a strange remark—all the more strange as it seems so utterly out of keeping with his naturally optimistic and buoyant nature: 'Actually I take no pleasure in all that has been done.' This must have been written in a rare moment of depression or perhaps of bodily and mental weariness.

Those who met the Abbot for the first time, or only saw him on rare occasions, might have thought him somewhat distant, not to say frigid: in reality he was neither haughty nor cold; but he certainly did not wear his heart on his sleeve. In one of his more revealing letters to the Abbess of Dourgne he wrote: 'I can love strongly—but I never say so. My love for you is as the love of a son for the noblest of mothers. It would have made me so happy had I felt able to tell you so.' This confession accounts for the reserve, the severe control of his feelings, which he practised at all times. In another letter to the same correspondent he writes: 'God has bestowed on me the gift of understanding the hearts of men and to respect their movements and their mysteries.' Not everybody would agree with this piece of self-portraiture. Some of his best friends would say that, notwithstanding his great wisdom and shrewdness joined to an extensive experience, he was not a good judge of character. This may or may not be a correct judgment—but it cannot be denied that more than once he was grievously mistaken in his estimate of men. It is certain that if he had been more willing to listen to counsel and warning he might have spared himself much pain and anxiety.

This book is not a panegyric—its subject needs none—for his place in monastic history and in the history of the Catholic Church in England is secure, but Abbot Anscar was only human. There is a story about Cromwell and a portrait painter which I actually heard from the Abbot's lips on more than one occasion. 'How do you wish to be painted?' the artist asked his terrible sitter. 'Warts and all,' was the gruff reply. Warts, if not too numerous or too prominent, are no great disfigurement—St Teresa of Avila had some, and so had Pope Pius XI —they may even impart a certain piquancy to a face. In any case a man's countenance is not judged by a couple of minor blemishes. In the present instance the 'warts' were but the defects of the Abbot's outstanding qualities. Dom Anscar was firmly convinced that his preservation from an untimely death in the waters of the Mediterranean was an assurance that Providence had singled him out for a twofold task, one in the material order, the other in the spiritual. In the execution of this twofold mission he exerted all his energies of mind and body; he even brought to it what, for lack of a better term, one might call a certain amount of ruthlessness. It is more than likely that he would not have achieved his purpose if he had felt bound to wait for the approval of a committee for his schemes as a builder, or for the concurrence of every individual member of the community in the changes he introduced in its way of life. St Benedict invests his abbot with an authority that must be described as absolute. True, in subsequent centuries, ecclesiastical legislation defined and limited this autocracy, but it has not deprived the head of a Benedictine monastery of personal authority and initiative. Of this right the Abbot of Buckfast made the fullest use at all times. Once his mind was made up he knew no hesitation and he would boldly override the objections of those who did not share his views—not to say his vision. In the domestic or purely monastic sphere in particular such methods were bound to create a certain amount of tension, and even to call forth opposition on the part of those who might be described as the conservative element and who not unnaturally resisted any break with tradition. Writing to the Abbess of Dourgne in March 1926, the Abbot said: 'It takes time to change old crusted ways and it is extremely difficult to overcome the prejudices of good people.' But he adds: 'We have done much already.' As a matter of fact he carried to a successful issue all the major items of the programme he had fixed for himself at the beginning of his rule. God manifestly blessed whatever he undertook, and the wonderful growth of the community, especially after the First World War, which, at one time, seemed destined to bring about its destruction, may surely be regarded as a manifest token of divine approval.

The Abbot's great gifts were seen at their best when he was able to plan on a big scale, when he had to solve knotty problems, or take a weighty decision. On the other hand, the petty details of day-to-day administration irked him, though it would not be correct to say that he neglected his duty in this respect. In the first years of his government in particular he gave close attention even to what could be regarded as the minutiae of administration, but a marked change occurred during the course of the last decade or so of his life. When on 25th August 1932, the consecration of the Abbey church brought the labour and toil, and likewise the excitement of twenty-four long years to a glorious climax, the Abbot's health was seriously impaired, though his intellectual powers remained as keen as ever. In those last years he devoted most of his time to literary work, to preaching and lecturing away from his abbey, with the inevitable result that he gave rather less attention to the task for which nature and grace had combined to equip him, I mean the moulding or fusing of a considerable group of men into a homogeneous body and setting before it a clearly-defined scope for its energies. In the material sphere he had achieved a brilliant success for which the world paid him its tribute of unstinted admiration; his task in the spiritual sphere was as yet unfinished and he was not given time to complete it.

It is idle to speculate what he might have done had length of days been added to the blessings Providence had so lavishly bestowed on him. With the completion of the Abbey church an exciting, all-absorbing interest had gone out of his life, yet, as his great friend of St Scholastica's in France had told him, his was 'the soul of a founder', and he loved and needed creative work. A trifling incident may be quoted here to confirm this impression. Not many days after the great ceremonies of the dedication, in the course of the short after-dinner walk which he invariably took with some of the Fathers, he suddenly stopped and observed that now the church was finished he was without a job: 'What shall I do?' he asked, with that peculiar smile of his which showed that he was not seriously perturbed by the prospect of idleness. 'Give yourself to a life of prayer,' someone suggested. 'An excellent suggestion,' he said with a smile. When I related this incident to the late Abbot Cabrol of Farnborough, the latter expressed astonishment at such freedom of speech: he evidently thought it was a poor joke, if not downright impertinence. However, Abbot Vonier was blessed with a sense of humour. As a matter of fact he declared there and then that he would begin by reading all the works of Cardinal Newman. He had already read the whole of Shakespeare and, more surprisingly, the entire literary output of Rudyard Kipling.[1]

While Dom Anscar's intellectual powers were of the highest order, some of nature's minor gifts had been dealt out to him in somewhat niggardly fashion. He had a keen sense of the beautiful in literature and in the arts; but it could not be said that his was an educated taste in such matters precisely because his taste was little more than ordinary good sense. It was fortunate that, on the whole, he left the architect a free hand in the planning of the church; but he interfered a good deal in the decorative part of the work, with the result that, in the opinion of men whose judgment commands respect, there are elements in the furniture and adornment of the building that are not in keeping with the austerity of its style. For a considerable time the architect offered strong and well-reasoned opposition to the high altar which is so

---

[1] He read a number of novels during this last period of his life—mostly such as have stood the test of time and which, perhaps, are no longer widely read, though they figure on many a bookshelf. But in this, as in all he did, he had a high purpose. Up to the very end he entertained the idea of writing a novel which would embody the great principles that dominated his own life—a novel, in other words, which would popularize the spiritual life. I have already referred to this ambition.

remarkable a feature of the church and which is rightly admired as one of the most beautiful products of the modern goldsmith's craft. In the end the Abbot had his way, but it was with not a little reluctance that the architect overcame his artistic and antiquarian scruples.

I have stressed the fact that there was nothing strained or narrow in Abbot Anscar's conception and personal practice of the spiritual life; on the contrary it was wide and spacious like Christianity itself. He was in every respect a perfectly natural human person. People who only saw him on formal occasions, or who only knew him from his books, or from having heard him preach or lecture, might have imagined him to be a somewhat solemn and perhaps rather forbidding person in private life and that his conversation must at all times have been about religious or theological subjects. Nothing could be further from the truth. He was far too wise not to realize that there is a time and place for everything. Hence, on a walk or at recreation, though never talkative, he was neither heavy nor morose, nor would he try to steer the conversation into pious or scholarly channels. In this he was happily at variance with the advice one had so often been given in French devotional books and by French retreat preachers—to the effect that one should somehow bring in, as it were edge-wise, a word about *le bon Dieu*. The Abbot thoroughly enjoyed a good story or a humorous remark; as a matter of fact he was quite happy to listen to the inconsequent chatter that constitutes the staple of most postprandial conversations. He had a real sense of humour and was quick to see the fun, or the absurdity, of a situation. Thus it was with a mischievous twinkle that he related how he had been asked by one good lady to call on her because she was anxious to have his guidance. She was reading the works of St John of the Cross but found it difficult to understand him. When the Abbot called he was shown into a splendidly furnished room where he found the student of the austere Carmelite's works reclining on a couch, divers means of refreshment being within easy reach. It only took Dom Anscar a few moments to understand why the good woman was unable to understand St John of the Cross.

Though personally highly disciplined in the matter of food and drink, he was by no means incapable of appreciating such things. The reader may remember a letter to his sister in which he lamented his having to superintend the kitchen. As Abbot he took considerable interest in that department for he was anxious that, within the limits of monastic moderation, not to say strictness, the community should be served with wholesome and appetizing food. A letter of his to the

Superior of the Convent of the Assumption in Paris, where his sister was in charge of the kitchen, throws a pleasing light on this facet of his many-sided personality. In the course of his repeated visits to the convent he had learnt to appreciate the high quality of the fragrant beverage which is the most pleasing ingredient of a French breakfast. He accordingly did not disdain to inquire into the secret of its production and even assisted at a practical demonstration by his sister. The upshot of it all was an order for the necessary apparatus to be sent to Buckfast. In his letter the Abbot wrote: 'The "tricolator" arrived this morning. The Brothers made a superb cup of coffee for me on the spot —they grasped the secret perfectly. A thousand thanks! Tell Sister Swithbert that the fragrance of the coffee they made for me (this morning) still clings to me. Now we begin to realize what good coffee is.'

The incident may seem too trivial to be recorded in these pages, but it is not without interest, for it shows that the builder, the voluminous writer and the eloquent orator was also a very human, genial and kindly person.

Another letter to the same Rev. Mother is in a very different tone. Mother Dolores was a Spaniard and the letter was written at the time of the terrible civil war when many thousands of priests, religious and ordinary Christians met with a cruel death at the hands of the communists. 'I am unable to shake off a feeling of sorrow,' he writes; 'you must be crushed beyond measure. I pray Our Lord to be your strength and comfort. We are back in the era of Martyrs, when the power of God's grace is more manifest than ever. The whole Church is concerned in this mystery of Christ's fight with Satan. You are yourself in the front rank of those who have to bear the brunt of this great battle. I pray much for you and I know that Sister Swithbert understands the depth of your distress. Already we Benedictines number many Martyrs in this conflict between the Lamb and the Red Dragon.'

It was not generally known, not even in his own community, that the Abbot had approached the British Government on behalf of the members of a Benedictine monastery in Spain. In a letter of 28th February 1937, he wrote to Mother Dolores: 'The British Government have promised me to do all in their power to secure the exit from Red Spain of a community of monks at present in prison, on condition that I keep them here until the end of the war. This promise I have given; pray that the plan may succeed.'

CHAPTER XIII

LAST YEARS AND DEATH

IN one of his delightful historical sketches Newman makes an observation which, at a first reading, strikes one as an unwarranted generalization. 'In what a little time,' the Cardinal writes, 'men move through the work which is, as it were, the end for which they were born, and which is to give a character to their names with posterity. They are known in history as the prime movers in this work, or as the instruments of that . . . and when we examine dates we often find that (what makes) them famous, lasted but a few years out of a long life' (*Historical Sketches*, Vol. II, p. 80).

It may be so, since the observation is made by so keen a student of history, but it is no less true that not a few of the great figures of history have enjoyed a long life and the achievements by which their names live were spread over a number of years. Newman himself lived to extreme old age and his work only ended with his life. Abbot Vonier, too, was granted all the time he needed for the realization of his great task, the work 'for which he was born', as Newman puts it, 'and which gives character to his name with posterity'. For all that, when we think of the magnitude of the undertaking to which he put his hand from the first days of his abbacy, and the slender resources available for its execution, even a period of thirty-two years must be reckoned as only 'a little time'.

When the first day of the year 1938 dawned upon the world Abbot Vonier had only recently kept his sixty-third birthday. He was undoubtedly looking forward to a number of such anniversaries, and though his health left much to be desired, there was apparently no cause for immediate anxiety. He was, however, a very tired man. Six years had gone by since the consecration of the church. During these years nothing happened of a nature to strike the public, but it would be absurd to imagine that they were altogether barren. In point of fact the Abbot displayed an intense activity during the last half-dozen years of his life. He travelled extensively and preached and lectured in various parts of the country and even on the Continent. It must be admitted that these extra-mural occupations seemed to monopolize his energy to such an extent as to distract his attention from his work within the precincts of the monastery. It would not be true to say that he had lost grip on the reins, but his hold was certainly relaxed. It was obvious that the routine administration of the house irked him, and while he was unwilling to delegate some of his authority, he himself was no longer able or willing to give to the details of administration the required attention. However, his prestige during these final years was greater than ever and he enjoyed the love and admiration of his religious family. They were proud of him, and his presence in their midst seemed to convey a sense of security and strength. With him to guide and inspire, one could look the future in the face with unshakable confidence.

In the early days of 1938—the last year of his life—Buckfast was detached from the French Province of the Cassinese Congregation and formally incorporated in the English Province. At the first chapter of the Province Abbot Anscar was appointed Visitor. He was the obvious choice for he was unquestionably the outstanding personality in the Province. The duties of a Visitor did not unduly tax his strength and he was a past master in solving problems expeditiously. All the same he had a heavy programme before him that year. He was far too cautious to commit himself so heavily, and so far in advance, if he had had any serious doubts about his ability to cope with so many engagements. As the year advanced one could not easily rid oneself of a suspicion that all was not well. By this time he had become exceedingly heavy. He also experienced some sharp attacks of gout. The first major engagement of the year was the above-mentioned Provincial chapter which was held at Ramsgate in the month of May. In July he went to Harrogate. He benefited by the cure, but there was no marked or permanent improvement in his general health. The fourth of August of that year—a day on which he could not help re-living his harrowing experience off the Spanish coast, thirty years before—the South-West experienced a thunderstorm of such violence, and such long duration, as even the oldest inhabitants could not remember. At times Abbey and church were literally enveloped in flames and, but for the highly efficient lightning-conductors only recently put up, incalculable damage would have been done for the church was repeatedly struck by lightning. At this time the central tower of the church was still completely encased in an elaborate wooden scaffolding; great damage would have been done if it had caught fire. Later in the day the Abbot confessed that he had been thoroughly frightened even though the awe-inspiring display of nature's violence had filled him with wonder and admiration for its Creator. A few days later, on the eve of the feast of the Assumption, he preached one of the most eloquent sermons of his whole career as a preacher. By this time the air was thick with rumours of war. Fear and anxiety gnawed at the hearts of millions and the nations were fast aligning themselves in opposite camps. The atmosphere was electric and it needed only a spark to set the world ablaze.

'What friendly nations are to each other,' the Abbot said that Sunday night, 'the Saints are for us Christians. Beyond the channel of time is the great people of the Saints, the company of many thousands of Angels, headed by their Queen, Our Blessed Lady. This intercourse with the Saints has stamped itself upon the history of nations, towns and villages. Traces of it remain everywhere. Since the Reformation the nations are deprived of this fellowship. For the worship of the Saints they have substituted hero-worship, the worship of mortal men, of the nation itself.' There was no mistaking who and what was meant. By this time Hitler had successfully cast an evil spell over a whole nation; a great people—or at least vast sections of it—hailed a skilful adventurer as a superman and to this apocalyptic figure of evil 'there was given a mouth speaking great things, and blasphemies', so that it came to pass, as the Book has it, that the nations were asking: 'Who shall be able to fight with him?' (Apoc. xiii. 4).

No one ever knew the Abbot so preoccupied as he was in those days when war—a world war—seemed imminent, for the second time in our lifetime. He watched events from day to day with absorbed attention. For many years he never, or hardly ever, read a newspaper—apart from *The Tablet*, but now he eagerly scanned *The Times* day by day and even went out into the village to listen to the B.B.C. news bulletins, for there was no radio set in the Abbey at that time. On 28th September he attended the opening of the recently completed church of St Thomas of Canterbury at Exeter. During the drive to the cathedral city he was more taciturn than ever. It was easy to perceive that he was labouring under very great distress. As soon as the ceremony was over we returned home with all speed, for gas-masks were to be handed out that evening. All through the service in the new church priests and people were oppressed by fear of what might be taking place at that very hour, and not only we, but the whole world was as it were holding its breath that afternoon, wondering what would be the issue of the momentous discussions at Berchtesgaden. Great was our relief when, as we drove into the Abbey grounds, one of our gardeners greeted us with the announcement that there would be no war. Opinions differ about the 'peace' secured at Munich, but the nations of Europe heaved an almost audible sigh of relief, and very sincere were the thanksgivings offered to God in every church and chapel of this and every civilized country on the following Sunday. We know how precarious the peace was, and at what price it was bought—but one may thank God that Abbot Anscar was spared the ordeal of another war—he had only another three months to live.

On 30th September the Abbey chronicler noted that 'Fr Abbot has an attack of gout. It started on Sunday, 25th September, but has increased since then.' This ominous entry was the first serious warning, but the Abbot recovered sufficiently to enable him to journey to London in order to sit for his portrait to Mr Simon Elwes. This full-length portrait has been exhibited in the Royal Academy, as well as in Paris and New York. The artist made us a present of it and it hangs in the south transept of the church—mainly because there is not sufficient wall-space anywhere else for so large a canvas. On 28th October the Abbot was once more in London when he gave an important address to a large gathering of Catholic Evidence Guild speakers. This was his last public appearance in London.[1]

From London the Abbot journeyed to Liverpool at the request of Archbishop Downey, his friend and admirer of many years. The two men were made to understand each other. In spite of very different temperaments they had a great deal in common—the one had but recently seen the completion of a great church, the other hoped to build an even bigger one, and neither of them was averse to any amount of publicity in a good cause. On the last Sunday of the month, the feast of Christ the King, which is also the titular of the future cathedral, the Abbot addressed a crowd of some four thousand people gathered for the annual cathedral rally.[2]

The Abbot had intended to return to Buckfast for the feast of All Saints, but owing to the installation of the heating system in the church a pontifical function on that day would have been difficult. So he decided to go from Liverpool to Paris, where he was to give a retreat to the monks of the Abbey of St Marie, rue de la Source. His sister's convent is within easy walking-distance of the abbey and thus brother and sister were able to meet daily for a whole week. From Paris the

---

[1] *Cf.* Chapter XI, p. 108.   [2] *Cf.* Chapter XI, p. 109.

Abbot went to the Abbey of St Martin, Ligugé, near Poitiers, for yet another retreat. Ligugé is one of the oldest monastic houses in Europe for its founder was none other than St Martin, the wonder-worker of the West, as St Nicholas is the wonder-worker of the East. On 11th November, the feast of St Martin and his own birthday, he preached a striking panegyric of the Saint which made a profound impression on his audience.[1] At the time of the Abbot's death the periodical published by the abbey paid this handsome tribute to his memory: 'Imbued as he was with a spirit that was wholly supernatural, he made it his life's aim to expound for his contemporaries the integral meaning of Christianity.' The writer then goes on: 'We would like to add . . . how greatly the monks of Ligugé appreciated the profound simplicity, charm and cheerfulness of their retreat preacher. He was unwilling to leave without saying good-bye to each one of us.' When one of the oldest of the lay brothers gave him rendezvous in heaven, he smilingly observed 'as for that there is no hurry'—'cela ne presse pas'.

By this time, even a strong and healthy man might have felt the need of at least a short rest, but the only respite the Abbot allowed himself was a stay of two or three days with Irish friends of his, Mr and Mrs Lalor, who owned a villa on the Riviera. From there he journeyed to Rome, where he was to lecture on the Benedictine apostolate as illustrated by St Augustine of Canterbury and the forty monks whom St Gregory dispatched from Rome for the spiritual conquest of Britain. A brilliant assembly, such as Rome alone can provide, listened to him on 28th November in the *Aula Magna* of the *Angelico*. He spoke in French. This lecture was his last public utterance.

A couple of days later the Abbot set out for the long homeward journey. This extensive and, in view of his health, exhaustive preaching and lecturing tour had been undertaken against medical advice—in fact, his doctor had done his utmost to dissuade him from embarking on it. But once Abbot Anscar had made up his mind, it would have required more than mere considerations of health to induce him to cancel an engagement. But the long-sustained effort had over-taxed his strength: he was exceedingly tired when he left the Eternal City. In the course of the journey he caught a chill, apparently during a short stay at Modena. He reached Buckfast on 6th December, still suffering from this cold. It was most fortunate that the great tower of the church had been freed from its encasing scaffolding only a few days before, so that on entering the Abbey grounds he had the satisfaction of behold-

[1] *Cf.* Chapter XI, p. 111.

ing the whole vast structure in all its beauty. Three days later a sharp attack of gout compelled him to take to his bed. This was the beginning of the end; from that day he never again set foot outside the house, and though he left his sick-room to receive the solemn profession of a choir monk and the perpetual vows of a lay brother, he was never again able to join the community either in church, refectory or recreation. The profession ceremony is a lengthy one, and though he did not attempt to sing the long prayers and the even longer preface, his breathing was painfully laboured, so much so indeed that more than one of those present felt extremely anxious, for there were moments when he appeared to be on the verge of a collapse.

On the following day symptoms of heart-trouble appeared, but his trusted and devoted physician did not take a grave view of his condition. He contented himself with prescribing complete rest. There could be no question, therefore, of the Abbot taking any part in the solemn offices of Christmas. Up to this year he had not once failed to officiate pontifically at all these great functions, and up to the very last he hoped to be able to do so on this occasion. On Christmas Eve a heart specialist was called in. The cardiograph and other tests were reassuring—there seemed to be no cause for alarm. For the community Christmas Day was overshadowed by the absence of the father of the family, even though there was no actual anxiety—all the more so as the medical report gave every hope that the patient would recover, provided he followed a strict diet and took a long rest. Fr Abbot spent his last Christmas on earth comfortably enough. During the Midnight Office on Christmas Eve he again and again asked the brother who attended him, 'What are they at now?' for he followed in spirit all the various functions of that holy night.

The Abbey chronicler notes that after Vespers, on Christmas Eve, he went to see Father Abbot, to wish him a happy Christmas and to sympathize with him for his inability to take part in the festivity. To this the Abbot replied: 'Oh! but I heard the bells! I loved listening to them!' and after a pause he added, 'How thankful and happy I am to be at home! Suppose I had been taken ill at Modena!'

That no one expected a fatal issue is shown by the fact that up to that very last day no mention had been made of the Last Sacraments, nor had the kindly doctor made any suggestion in that sense. Though not a Catholic, Dr Williams knew quite well what the Last Sacraments mean to Catholics and, as he told me more than once, he made a great point of warning those whom it concerned as soon as he saw that there was danger of death. When therefore, in the early hours of Boxing Day, the community was informed of the death of their beloved Abbot, the shock was such that, at first, one could scarcely believe one's own ears. The events of that sad morning have been recorded both by the Abbey chronicler and by the infirmarian and what follows is a summary of their story.

Shortly after five o'clock on the morning of the 26th, Dom Martin Griffin entered the sick-room to make sure that all was ready for the Abbot's Communion and to light the two candles. At five-thirty the infirmarian took Holy Communion to Fr Abbot as he had done every morning for some time. The sick man appeared to be his usual self and, as always at that time, absorbed in prayer and deep recollection. A little later the infirmarian returned with a cup of hot milk. This the Abbot took and, with a nod, dismissed the infirmarian. The latter, however, observed that perhaps he had better stay—to remove the additional pillow that supported him—but the Abbot told him he could manage quite well. These were his last words.

An hour or so later the brother who had had the care of his room for many years came up to light the fire. When he entered, the Abbot seemed to be asleep—his eyes were closed, the head slightly turned sideways, the arms folded and the hands resting on his chest—his usual position when asleep. During the preceding weeks he had invariably gone to sleep after drinking a cup of milk. On Christmas Day he had told the infirmarian how well he slept at that hour, so well indeed that he did not wake up when the brother came to light the fire. We may, therefore, presume that on that day too he was asleep between seven and seven-thirty, the time when the brother left the room. The latter had not switched on the electric light, so as not to disturb the Abbot's sleep. At eight o'clock Dom Martin Griffin returned to the sick-room. At first he too thought that Fr Abbot was sleeping. But after a while the uncanny stillness and the sight of the dropped jaw filled him with apprehension. He then felt the Abbot's pulse. This confirmed his fears —there was no pulse. After a brief prayer he left the room, when he met Brother Ignatius. To him he broke the news, telling him to telephone for the doctor. At that moment one of the Fathers came along; he, on hearing the news, hurried to the sacristy to get the Holy Oil. He anointed Fr Abbot, using the short formula. By this time the sad news had spread through the house like wildfire and a number of the brethren gathered round their dead father and recited the prayers for the dying. Dr Williams, obviously deeply affected by this sudden death of one for whom he cherished the greatest regard, declared that Fr Abbot had certainly died in his sleep since the eyes were closed and there was no trace of a struggle, no contortions of the face, and the arms had remained folded as in sleep. It would seem that the heart stopped at about eight o'clock, the cause of death being coronary thrombosis. The clot that put so sudden an end to our revered Abbot's life could not have formed before the previous night for on Christmas Eve two cardiographs had been taken by Dr Gibson, a heart specialist, and the blood-pressure had likewise been tested. The presence of a clot was completely ruled out since the graphs could not have failed to reveal it. The clot must have formed in the course of the last night for there had been a visible improvement in the patient's condition.

On the day following Christmas the Church honours the first Martyr, St Stephen. Some years previous to this day the feast had fallen on a Sunday, when the Abbot preached, his text being the Proto-martyr's words: 'Behold, I see the heavens opened and the Son of man standing on the right hand of God' (Acts viii. 55). Now, in the early hours of St Stephen's day, Fr Abbot was awakened from his peaceful slumber, not by the return of daylight, but by the splendour of the countenance of Him whom he had served so faithfully, loved so ardently, of whom he had spoken and written so copiously—awakened not to another day of this earthly life but to the light and life of that day which knows no end, for its light radiates from the eternal Sun of righteousness.

'The state of death,' the Abbot had written, 'is only another phase of our spiritual incorporation in Christ . . . the Christian's death is a membership in that most adorable mystery, Christ's death. Therefore life and death for the Christian are merely two phases of the same glorious event—our life in Christ—embracing both the state of the living and the state of death.' Then, quoting St Paul, Rom. xiv. 9, 'to this end Christ died and rose again, that he might be Lord both of the dead and of the living', he went on: 'This clearly supports my con-tention that the Apostle considers the state of death as another phase of life. Christ's dominion over the dead is a dominion of graciousness over positive, living, conscious beings, as much as His dominion over the living; not a power over vague shadows, or distant memories, or unconscious personalities' (*Coll. Works*, I, 60).

The day was a bank holiday and there was no telephone in the Abbey, so most of the Abbot's friends heard of our loss through the B.B.C.'s news bulletins. Their grief, not to say their consternation, was all the greater as nothing had prepared them for the shock, neither a long illness nor advanced age, since the Abbot had only recently entered upon his sixty-fourth year.

There was a general feeling that the only fit resting-place for the Abbot's mortal remains was the church, his outstanding achievement in the material sphere. Permission to this effect was readily granted by the Home Office, but, on the other hand, in the excitement of the hour, the monks completely overlooked a ruling of canon law which only permits the burial within a church of bishops and abbots *nullius*, that is, abbots wielding episcopal jurisdiction over territory around their abbey. As for the Home Office permission, we subsequently learnt that since the church had been used for burial before this, viz. prior to the year 1539! only the county and local medical officer's permit was required. How Abbot Anscar would have rejoiced over such an instance of continuity! Thus even in death he constituted a link between the old and the new Buckfast. He himself had never expressed any wish concerning his burial—he certainly wished to rest among his brethren in the Abbey cemetery. His grave is on the gospel side of the high altar. No spot in the whole edifice could be a more appropriate resting-place for one who loved the Eucharist so ardently and wrote about it so admirably. There he rests, within earshot of 'the murmur of the Mass' and the tinkling of the sacring-bell, until the great awakening on the world's last day.

It fell to the Abbot of Prinknash to give voice to the thoughts and emotions of the vast congregation that had gathered for the funeral. The preacher paid a moving tribute to the late Abbot, of whom he said that 'if he was anything at all, he was a great Churchman'. Another passage of the discourse may be quoted because it is an admirable assessment of Abbot Vonier's personality: 'His was the simple faith of a child,' the preacher said, 'combined with the faith of a great intellect, and one of the most beautiful things in the world, and one of the most powerful, is that of a great mind controlled by a great faith.'

From the hour when the B.B.C. informed the outside world of our immense loss, hundreds of messages of sympathy reached the community from every corner of the country. They constitute a wonderful tribute of admiration and gratitude to the Abbot, whose personality and written and spoken word had meant so much to so many. Only a few quotations can be given here, but they may help the reader to form a clearer picture of the subject of this book than its compiler has been able to draw.

One of the most striking of these tributes appeared in the periodical published by the monks of St Augustine's Abbey, Ramsgate. The writer was none other than Abbot Adrian Taylor, who was particularly qualified to appreciate the late Abbot. This is what he wrote a few weeks after the funeral: 'Much has been written about Abbot Vonier's achievement as scholar, as preacher, as writer, and above all as the restorer of his ancient abbey—but his greatest achievement was his own personality. During his thirty-two years as Abbot of Buckfast he stood forth before the world primarily as a man of God, as the fine flower of monastic culture, as a man whose life was in itself an object-lesson in Catholic spirituality. When we assisted at his burial in the chancel of the church which he had built, we were aware of the passing of one of the most eminent men of our time' (*The Thanet Catholic Gazette*, January 1939).

One of the monks of Ampleforth wrote: 'The Fathers here were exceedingly distressed to hear of your great Abbot's death. . . . We were saying today what untold good had been done by his books. As our Prior put it: "he recalled the modern world to sane and solid spirituality". I know this to be true from the help they [the books] have given to many to whom I have recommended them. It is certainly true of myself. I shall never forget the retreat he gave us at Ampleforth in 1923. It was a landmark for many of us—in particular I recall his discourse on the simplicity and prosaic circumstances of the death of many good souls which he contrasted with the artificial dramatization of it in so much hagiography. How his own end exemplifies his words.'

Don Sturzo, a frequent and well-loved guest in our Abbey, wrote: '*Che bel tipo!* I have never met such greatness and such greatness of heart: we must for ever thank God.'

A final quotation is taken from the secular press. In the *Daily Telegraph*, 'Peterborough' wrote: 'Not long ago I had lunch with Anscar Vonier, the late Abbot of Buckfast, in the refectory of the Abbey. . . . I sat on his right and admired the sparkling ring on his finger and the dignified gestures of his hands. . . . Afterwards we retired to his study, where coffee was served. This was black and exceptionally strong. The Abbot told me it was made according to a recipe of his own'. (This was, of course, the recipe taught him by his sister, *cf.* p. 139.) 'He spoke quietly, weighing every word. . . . The one thing he hoped for, the Abbot told me, was to see the Abbey completed, a task he had set himself some thirty years ago. "Once the church is completed and the whole building finished" (he must have had the domestic buildings in mind) "I have done my task and I can go".' This conversation is of interest on account of the light it throws on the Abbot's own view of his work.

I may be permitted to reproduce, by way of conclusion, some things I wrote years ago, while still stunned by the abrupt termination of a career which, by the law of averages, might have continued for at least another decade. As we have seen in an earlier chapter, the Abbot's first teachers were the Fathers of the Holy Ghost at Beauvais. Is it a mere coincidence that throughout his life a special devotion to the Third Person of the Blessed Trinity was an outstanding characteristic of his spiritual life? His last book, *The Spirit and the Bride*, which some regard as his best, is chiefly concerned with the Person of the Holy Spirit. His very first sermon was on this theme. It was delivered, not in church but in the refectory, during the midday meal and as an exercise in the art of public speaking, for he was not yet a priest. The setting was not inspiring and the audience's attention was necessarily divided, for even monks take some interest in their dinner. However, even after the lapse of more than fifty years I can see the youthful orator, pale and lean as he then was, nervously clutching the corners of the reader's desk, or from time to time making some rather gawky gesture with his hands. But the discourse made a profound impression on many of the listeners.

Grave, thoughtful, at times almost solemn, Dom Anscar put in practice from his early years St Benedict's somewhat ungrammatically worded injunction to his monks, in the forty-second chapter of his Rule: *Omni tempore silentium debent studere monachi*—Monks should love and practise silence at all times. Dom Anscar spoke several languages fluently, but he could hold his tongue in all of them. I remember his saying that he was never happier than when completely alone with his own thoughts; that he would be perfectly content on a lonely island, even without a book. Yet by a strange anomaly he spoke a great deal, and loved it; in fact, he would not have remained for long on a lonely island for he was far too eager to share with others the beautiful thoughts that came to him during those characteristic and at times disconcerting silences of his. He loathed mere chatter but delighted in preaching and lecturing.

There was an old-world courtesy in his speech and he thoroughly disliked the easy informality which is so marked a feature of present-day social intercourse. He loved the land of his adoption with a deep affection; in fact, his love for England was all the stronger for being a reasoned choice and no mere instinctive attachment due to the accident of birth. One so clear-sighted as he could not fail to appreciate the providential mission of the British Empire in this modern world—a mission comparable only to that of Rome's Empire at the beginning of the Christian era. He was proud of his British citizenship and accordingly saw to it that those of his monks who were of foreign birth should enjoy the same privilege. He obviously felt a great reverence for the person of the King. When speaking of him—or of the Queen—he almost invariably used the formula 'His', or 'Her Majesty'.

When he built the great Abbey church, he did not do so for show. The edifice was meant to be an object-lesson of what the Catholic Church stands for: a reminder of the rights and claims of God. The lofty tower was to be a finger pointing to man's true home. He loved the crowds that came to see the church, and the facilities for sight-seeing offered to them he regarded as an apostolic activity.

Abbot Anscar's was a many-sided personality, but he was essentially and before all else a monk. He had a unique grasp of the ethos of the Benedictine life. He loved and cherished all the big and little things that make up the tapestry of the monastic day. Indulgent, condescending, compassionate, he readily dispensed others from this or that arduous duty—as for instance the long night-office; he was exacting only with himself. When eventually the night-office came to be said at a less difficult hour, viz. in the early morning, he would be in his stall even if he had only just returned from a journey or an exacting engagement. This is not to say that he could not be strict when there was a call for sternness. In the first years of his rule he was perhaps somewhat exacting. He did not spare himself and accordingly felt he had a right to require others to give of their best at all times.

At the time of his death Abbot Anscar, though only in his sixty-fourth year, was one of the oldest abbots of the Order. There were many who felt that there was not his like among contemporary Benedictines. Not only for his own community, but for a vast number of men and women beyond the monastic boundaries, he had been a sure guide, an inspiring teacher, an oracle whose answers to any questions, brief and terse as they were, were invariably luminous and to the point. For more than three decades we had taken him for granted, as one takes for granted the common air, the daily bread, or the changes of the seasons. For more than thirty years he had stood in our midst, like a mighty oak in the forest. With little warning, or none at all, he suddenly crashed to the ground as the giant of the forest is felled by the axe of the woodman. For one who had ever viewed all things *sub specie aeternitatis*, what was our immense loss was gain incomparable. Christ, Our Lord, than whom he had held nothing dearer, as St Benedict bids us in the prologue to his Rule, had come to call for him and in the brightness of His approach His faithful servant opened his eyes and awoke to the light that is life.

INDEX